NEW DIRECTIONS FOR COMMUNITY COLLEGES

Arthur M. Cohen
EDITOR-IN-CHIEF

Florence B. Brawer
ASSOCIATE EDITOR

Paula Zeszotarski
PUBLICATION COORDINATOR

How Community Colleges Can Create Productive Collaborations with Local Schools

James C. Palmer
Illinois State University

EDITOR

Number 111, Fall 2000

JOSSEY-BASS
San Francisco

ERIC®

Clearinghouse for Community Colleges

HOW COMMUNITY COLLEGES CAN CREATE PRODUCTIVE COLLABORATIONS WITH LOCAL SCHOOLS
James C. Palmer (ed.)
New Directions for Community Colleges, no. 111
Volume XXVIII, number 3
Arthur M. Cohen, Editor-in-Chief
Florence B. Brawer, Associate Editor

New Directions for Community Colleges is indexed in Current Index to Journals in Education (ERIC).

Microfilm copies of issues and articles are available in 16mm and 35mm, as well as microfiche in 105mm, through University Microfilms Inc., 300 North Zeeb Road, Ann Arbor, Michigan 48106-1346.

ISSN 0194-3081   ISBN 0-7879-5428-4

NEW DIRECTIONS FOR COMMUNITY COLLEGES is part of The Jossey-Bass Higher and Adult Education Series and is published quarterly by Jossey-Bass Inc., 350 Sansome Street, San Francisco, California 94104-1342, in association with the ERIC Clearinghouse for Community Colleges. Periodicals postage paid at San Francisco, California, and at additional mailing offices. POSTMASTER: Send address changes to New Directions for Community Colleges, Jossey-Bass Inc., 350 Sansome Street, San Francisco, California 94104-1342.

SUBSCRIPTIONS cost $60.00 for individuals and $107.00 for institutions, agencies, and libraries. Prices subject to change.

THE MATERIAL in this publication is based on work sponsored wholly or in part by the Office of Educational Research and Improvement, U.S. Department of Education, under contract number ED-99-CO-0010. Its contents do not necessarily reflect the views of the Department or any other agency of the U.S. Government.

EDITORIAL CORRESPONDENCE should be sent to the Editor-in-Chief, Arthur M. Cohen, at the ERIC Clearinghouse for Community Colleges, University of California, 3051 Moore Hall, Box 951521, Los Angeles, California 90095-1521. All manuscripts receive anonymous reviews by external referees.

Cover photograph © Rene Sheret, After Image, Los Angeles, California, 1990.

Printed in the United States of America on acid-free recycled paper containing 100 percent recovered waste paper, of which at least 20 percent is postconsumer waste

CONTENTS

Editor's Notes

Community colleges have long since separated themselves administratively from local school districts. But the schools and the colleges remain thoroughly intertwined, if only by the steady flow of students from grade 12 to grade 13. Just over half of the first-time students who begin postsecondary studies at a community college do so within twelve months of their high school graduation; 74 percent are under the age of twenty-four (Kojaku and Nuñez, 1999). The academic success of these students at the community college depends on their preparation in the schools. And the schools depend on the colleges to provide many of their students with the opportunity for advancement in the graded system of education, which may lead to further study at a university, employment, or both.

The chapters in this volume consider the administrative and policy implications of this interdependency, focusing primarily on ways of establishing and sustaining collaborative work between the colleges and local school districts. Chapters One and Two consider factors that sometimes impede collaboration between colleges and schools. Katherine Boswell examines state policy in Chapter One, noting how the administrative separation of the schools and the colleges works against expectations for the creation of seamless K–16 systems. She considers state policy options for closing this administrative divide. In Chapter Two, Al Azinger examines this divide from the perspective of the local school district. He draws on his long experience as a school superintendent to question the extent to which school administrators view collaboration with community colleges as a means of addressing those issues that drive administrative action in local school districts.

Subsequent chapters focus on the varying types of college-school collaboration and on implications for student service departments. Debra D. Bragg examines tech-prep programming in Chapter Three, noting what the history of tech-prep teaches about the requisites of success for joint work between colleges and schools. Hans A. Andrews turns to concurrent enrollment in Chapter Four, drawing on his own experience as a chief academic officer to examine the administration of programs that allow high school students to enroll in college courses. Chapter Five, by Cecilia L. Cunningham and Chery S. Wagonlander, focuses on the middle school high schools operated by community colleges for at-risk students. The authors, who administer middle college high schools at Mott Community College and LaGuardia Community College, respectively, offer advice on what is required to initiate and sustain these unique secondary schools. In Chapter Six, Lemuel W. Watson considers joint college-school actions that can ease student transition from school to college.

Next, Chapters Seven and Eight provide case studies of school-college collaboration. Both chapters were written jointly by community college and school educators. In Chapter Seven, Charlene R. Nunley, Mary Kay Shartle-Galotto, and Mary Helen Smith describe how Maryland's Montgomery College works with local schools to help prepare students for college-level work. In Chapter Eight, May Kuang-chi Chen, James L. Konantz, M. Lucia Rosenfeld, and Clara Frost describe the varying ways in which Los Angeles Trade Technical College works with surrounding schools that serve urban, underserved populations.

The last three chapters provide additional information from a variety of perspectives. In Chapter Nine, Elizabeth T. Lugg discusses the legal problems that can emerge when community colleges enroll high school students. She also describes the strategies that community college administrators can undertake to avoid potential legal problems. In Chapter Ten, I review the demographic and policy trends that underscore the importance of this joint work. These trends include projected increases in the number of young people emerging from the schools, as well as a growing tendency to link school reform with student preparation for college in so-called K–16 systems. Both underscore the importance of administrative initiatives that strengthen the community college role as an extension of local schools. Finally, Chapter Eleven, by Charles L. Outcalt, provides a bibliography of ERIC resources with further information on the administration of school-college collaborative efforts.

Taken together, the chapters illustrate key administrative challenges that those who would bridge the school and community college bureaucracies face. Linking these bureaucracies for the sake of educational opportunity remains an ongoing task, made necessary by the community college's unique role as an institution standing between the schools on the one hand and the universities or the labor market on the other.

James C. Palmer
Editor

Reference

Kojaku, L. K., and Nuñez, A.-M. *Descriptive Summary of 1995–96 Beginning Postsecondary Students with Profiles of Students Entering 2- and 4-Year Institutions.* Washington, D.C.: U.S. Department of Education, Office of Educational Research and Improvement, 1999. (ED 425 684)

JAMES C. PALMER *is associate professor in the Department of Educational Administration and Foundations, Illinois State University.*

1

In the past, different governance structures and assessment standards separated community college and K–12 systems and impaired the effectiveness of the educational system. New state and federal policies are opening the way to successful collaborations between educational sectors.

Building Bridges or Barriers? Public Policies That Facilitate or Impede Linkages Between Community Colleges and Local School Districts

Katherine Boswell

To accomplish the quantum changes needed in higher education, we need new forms of leadership. In particular, we need to examine our existing framework of higher education policies to take down the barriers and provide the direction to allow us to reach that potential.

Governor Paul E. Patton, Kentucky, Education Commission of the States, State Education Leader

Kentucky Governor Patton echoes the concerns of many other state policymakers who are calling for the creation of more seamless approaches to public education at all levels. With the growing recognition that 70 percent of all high school graduates go on to some level of postsecondary education, policymakers are deeply concerned about the barriers that stand in the way of students' moving smoothly from high school to college. In a recent poll of legislators conducted by the Education Commission of the States and the National Conference of State Legislatures, 71 percent of the respondents placed a "very high" priority on creating greater K–16 collaboration.

However, because different governance structures typically oversee K–12 and higher education, the creation of such integrated K–16 systems may require external policy leadership at the state level. Governors, legislators, and their staff increasingly are committed to undertaking these efforts

NEW DIRECTIONS FOR COMMUNITY COLLEGES, no. 111, Fall 2000 © Jossey-Bass, a Wiley company

as part of education reform movements underway across the nation. Community colleges, with their reputation as open-access, learner-centered institutions, are being identified by policymakers in an increasing number of states as the sector best suited to bridge the perceived barriers between K–12 and postsecondary education.

The Great Divide

The United States is unique in its emphasis on local control of public education at every level. Scholars suggest that American K–12 and higher education systems are among the world's least-linked education structures. Unlike most other countries, the United States does not have a central ministry of education with the authority to dictate a national curriculum or set standards for either the K–12 system or public colleges and universities. Michael Kirst of Stanford University argues that historic attempts to provide mass education at both levels have resulted in significant disconnects between K–12 and college faculties, curricula, and standards (*Education Reform,* 1999).

However, in contrast to universities, community colleges and K–12 systems have had much in common, at least historically. In the early decades of the twentieth century, "junior" colleges were organized in many states to provide grades 13 and 14 under the auspices and authority of local school districts. It was not until the 1960s that states began moving governance of two-year college systems from state boards of education to postsecondary coordinating and governing boards. Currently, twenty-nine states align their community colleges in a common postsecondary system with four-year universities and colleges, and sixteen states have created independent state community college governing or coordinating boards. Only six states continue to place primary authority for governance or coordination of their community colleges with the state board of education (Education Commission of the States, 1997; Center for Community College Policy, 2000).

K–12 origins are also reflected in the eighteen states where trustee candidates for local community college boards still stand for general election, much like members of local school boards. However, thirty-four states have adopted a governance model more typical of universities, with community college board members appointed by the governor or legislature. (Only three states elect members of their university governing boards.) Like K–12 districts, locally governed community colleges typically have the authority to levy at least some level of local taxes, while community colleges with appointed boards are much more likely to get the bulk of their operating support from the state, as public universities do.

Despite these common origins and a tradition of being open-door rather than selective institutions, community colleges over the years have become much more like four-year colleges than secondary schools, adopting much of the academic culture traditionally associated with universities.

Different funding mechanisms and governance patterns contribute to the perception that two-year colleges are competitors of rather than collaborators with K–12 systems for scarce state and local resources.

Policymakers increasingly believe that these differences are creating roadblocks for students who are seeking to move between systems, and political pressure is growing to overcome these disconnects. Recognizing the need in a highly competitive world economy for a well-educated citizenry with some postsecondary education or training, elected officials are leading efforts to create K–16 systems that overcome the traditional turf battles that have existed between K–12 systems and postsecondary education. They are tired of finger pointing on the part of different sectors, each blaming the other for students who have fallen through the cracks between systems and left school ill prepared and without the technical skills to get a good job.

Evidence of the Disconnect Between Schools and Colleges

Evidence of the significant disconnect between high schools and colleges is illustrated in a number of incongruities between institutional policies and practices. In particular, the difference between high school graduation standards and college admission requirements has become a concern among policymakers. In their final years of high school, students typically take state assessment tests composed of multiple-choice questions reflecting skills taught between middle school and lower high school. However, because these tests are not used to determine college admission, students are required to take one or more college admissions tests (like the American College Test or Scholastic Aptitude Test) that often cover content not included on K–12 assessments. When students arrive at the college or university, they are administered still a third set of tests to measure their academic preparation for placement into college courses. These exams often cover content not included in either of the previous examinations and require students to do significant amounts of writing for the first time. This system of uncoordinated tests and requirements can create significant barriers for students, particularly for poor and minority students who are most likely to come from high schools that do not do a good job of preparing students for college success ("Ticket to Nowhere," Fall 1999).

There is evidence of other disconnects in public education policy as well. For example, while many K–12 schools are changing dramatically because of the standards-based education reform movement, many colleges and universities continue to operate in the traditional way and are ill prepared to meet the anticipated needs of students educated in a standards-based K–12 environment. And there is an assumption that the responsibility of K–12 teachers ends with college admissions rather than college success, while the responsibility of higher education begins with the admission process rather than any significant involvement in the preparation of students up to that point.

Advanced placement courses and private testing networks like the American College Test and the Scholastic Aptitude Test (which are not well aligned with K–12 standards or assessments) have come the closest to setting national standards for college admissions (*Education Reform,* 1999).

Finally, reports indicate that 41 percent of all first-time community college freshmen and 29 percent of all first-time college freshmen require some remediation prior to entry into college-level work (U.S. Department of Education, 1996).

Building Bridges Between Systems

Historically, K–12 and postsecondary boards have operated independently from one another. Separate governance, funding systems, and regulatory requirements contribute to education policy made in isolation. However, many college presidents, in partnership with high school principals and superintendents, recognize this disconnect and are promoting programs that encourage greater school-college collaboration and are providing resources to fund bridge programs that help prepare more students for college.

A recent report, *Statewide School-College (K–16) Partnerships to Improve School Performance* (Tafel and Eberthart, 1999), argues that if education leaders and state policymakers want to meet their goals for educational improvement and enhanced student achievement, current structures and practices need to be reconceived and new systemic approaches need to be identified. Such strategies might include early outreach and preparation for college, a focus on improved teacher quality, and the development of standards, competencies, and assessments across education sectors, as well as operational issues such as coordination and articulation of programs, communication of services, funding streams, and improved data collection.

One of the principal challenges facing states is to help community colleges and universities align their own policies and practices with current K–12 reforms. Jan Somerville, director of state systems, K–16, for the University System of Maryland, has been quoted as saying that although increasing numbers of states are encouraging school-college collaboration, it is still "a radical act at the state level to think K–16" (Ruppert, 1999, p. 11). State policymakers need to step up their efforts to promote collaboration and cooperation between K–12 and higher education if the goals of seamless systems are to be achieved.

Langenberg suggests that the strongest state-level K–16 partnerships are emerging in states in which there is a statewide system of colleges and universities that is a natural counterpart of the state's department of education. These partners can recruit colleges, business and community leaders, and others to grapple jointly with the problem ("Reforming Both Houses," 1997).

Under the aegis of the National Association of System Heads (NASH), an overarching goal for K–16 was developed and signed by a group of chief state school officers and higher education leaders:

> We aim to achieve in each of our states levels of performance by all students at elementary, secondary and postsecondary levels that meet or exceed rigorous and realistic standards. These standards will need to be dynamic, changing and increasing, as necessary to reflect the changing needs of a globally competitive knowledge-based economy and society. In pursuing this goal, we will work to eliminate all significant performance gaps among students from different economic classes, genders, races, or ethnic groups ["Reforming Both Houses," 1997, p. 3].

At a later meeting these education CEOs concluded:

> Our nation is no longer well served by an education system that prepares a few to attend college to develop their minds for learned pursuits while the rest are expected only to build their muscles for useful labor. In the twenty-first century, all students must meet higher achievement standards in elementary, secondary, and postsecondary schools and thus be better prepared for the challenges of work and citizenship ["Ticket to Nowhere," 1999, p. 3].

State Policy Options to Encourage School-College Collaboration

Institutional leaders and state policymakers interested in building seamless systems might consider some policy options.

Alignment of Assessment and Admissions

States should consider bringing their course requirements for high school graduation in line with their standards as well as college admissions requirements.

Virtually all state standards for high school seniors include knowledge of geometry and algebra, but only thirteen states require students to take those courses. However, even bringing graduation requirements in line with standards does not solve the problem if those standards do not align with college expectations. Only two states, Oklahoma and Tennessee, have attempted to line the two up, thereby increasing the chance that high school graduates will be prepared for college-level work. In most states, according to the Education Trust, there is no such alignment ("Ticket to Nowhere," 1999).

The typical state requires high school graduates to complete two or three years of mathematics. Students who take Algebra 1, Geometry, and Algebra 2 will meet graduation requirements while also fulfilling prerequisites for community college and university credit–bearing courses. However, the student who takes such courses as Consumer Math or Review of Arithmetic will meet the requirements for high school graduation but not the requirements for college admission. Similar issues exist with high school science classes that do not include laboratory work or English classes that require little or no writing ("Ticket to Nowhere," 1999).

> Community colleges and high schools must do a better job of identifying and communicating to students and their parents the academic skills needed to prepare for postsecondary education.

Critics of community colleges argue that the mere existence of "second-chance" open-door institutions has encouraged students to take demanding college admissions standards lightly. Nevertheless, even at open-door community colleges, admission to more competitive programs, such as nursing or physical therapy, is more difficult than gaining admission to many four-year colleges. And although students may be admitted with inadequate credentials, the first thing they will confront at the community college will be the requirement to take a placement test that requires them to have college-level skills such as Algebra 2 or beyond ("Ticket to Nowhere," 1999).

> States should consider administering K–12 assessments through the eleventh grade and using that score for placement at community colleges and four-year campuses. They also should provide incentives that will help colleges and universities align their own policies and practices with current K–12 reform.

There are no consequences or incentives for secondary students to take state assessment tests seriously. Too often these are multiple choice exams with no mechanism to measure writing skills. Students enter college, do poorly on placement tests, and end up in remediation (*Education Reform,* 1999). By providing incentives to colleges to align their admissions and placement policies with state standards, significant individual and state resources could be saved and redirected to other educational investments.

State Efforts to Reduce Remediation

> Reducing the need for remediation at two- and four-year colleges will happen only when state and institutional leaders work together across systems to identify and create solutions to overcome the causes of poor student preparation.

When Arkansas determined that K–12 curriculum and instruction were major factors in the poor preparation of students for college, the state established a statewide professional development program in math, science, and reading that reached 85 percent of K–12 teachers in the state. There has been an 11 percent drop in the number of entering college freshmen needing remediation in the six years since the program was instituted (Crowe, 1998).

High school graduation tests and postsecondary "rising junior tests," which require a student to demonstrate mastery of remedial courses and related subject area exams, have been adopted by Texas and Florida and are being considered in many other states. Arizona gives students one year to correct deficiencies, while Georgia requires passing an exit exam within four quarters of enrollment.

Some states have chosen to be proactive in providing incentives aimed at reducing the need for remediation and increasing the number of students who go on to postsecondary education. Several states provide incentives to students to take a full set of core courses and maintain a certain grade point average. For example, the Academic Challenges Scholarship program in Arkansas rewards students who take a full set of core courses. The percentage of Arkansas high school graduates completing these courses before entering college grew from 41 percent in 1991 to 73 percent in 1997 (Crowe, 1998).

Curriculum Alignments/2+2 Programs

State policymakers should ensure that vocational and technical programs are well integrated between K–12, community colleges, universities, and workforce development efforts.

Vocational and technical programs at high schools and area vocational schools are too often poorly integrated with community college and workforce development efforts, and, in many cases, have not kept current with the technical requirements of the modern economy. Many traditional vocational courses are still taught based on the industrial model using clock hours rather than credit hours, making it difficult or impossible for students who choose to go on to associate or baccalaureate programs to transfer their credits. Similarly, many universities are resistant to allowing articulation of associate of applied science (A.A.S.) degrees with applied technical baccalaureate programs, limiting the opportunity for a student who completes an applied associate degree to pursue a four-year degree.

Student Information Tracking Systems

States should support the development of computerized information systems that will allow students to be tracked through the K–12 system, into postsecondary education at both two- and four-year colleges, and then into the workforce, while adequately ensuring individual privacy.

With the growing interest and emphasis on accountability, many states are requiring schools and colleges to report publicly on the success of graduates, sometimes as a significant factor in performance funding or budgeting efforts. However, the lack of common student information systems to track and monitor the progress of individuals as they move through the education system makes those efforts difficult or impossible. Incompatible data systems impede community colleges from reporting back to an individual high school on the achievements of its graduates, and it is often difficult to track the performance of community college students who transfer to a university or leave the college and seek employment.

These reporting efforts are further complicated by conflicting state and federal regulations protecting student privacy while also ensuring a student's right to know completion rates of prior students enrolled in any vocational or technical program. States need to assess the effectiveness and quality of conflicting state and federal regulations to establish systems that will balance the right to privacy with accountability requirements.

Dual/Concurrent Enrollment

State policymakers should fund the dual/concurrent enrollment of upper-division high school students in community college courses and provide incentives to students to accelerate their educational progress.

Demographers predict a significant increase in the number of high school graduates who will be seeking opportunities for higher education over the next decade. Children of the baby boom generation, also known as Tidal Wave II, will have a significant impact on college enrollments in many regions of the country, particularly across the West and South. This demand for college access on top of the increasing numbers of adults who will be returning to higher education for additional education or retraining is projected to strain the capacity of colleges and universities.

Encouraging qualified high school students to concurrently enroll in college credit courses not only helps bridge the gap between high school and college, but makes the senior year, often considered a time for fun and games by graduating students, more productive. Dual-enrollment credits also help students progress faster through their college education, saving the state and themselves money, while freeing up opportunities for other students.

Utah now offers any student who earns an associate degree within three months of high school graduation (through any combination of advanced placement, summer, or concurrent enrollment credits) a full tuition state scholarship for their upper-division college work.

Nonetheless, political support for dual-enrollment programs is not universal. Concurrent enrollment in Arizona has come under fire by the state budget office because of the charge that Arizona taxpayers are paying twice since both the community college and K–12 system receive state support for the enrolled student. In addition, other problems exist. For instance, questions are sometimes raised about the academic quality of concurrent enrollment programs, and many universities refuse to recognize dual-enrollment transfer credits.

Early Identification and Intervention Programs

State policymakers and college leaders should adopt measures that will identify and provide supplemental programs to at-risk students at a much earlier age, to help prepare them for postsecondary success.

The Georgia Postsecondary Readiness Enrichment Program (PREP) offers supplemental programs for students in grades 7–12 with the goal of improving their access to and success in postsecondary education. Arkansas and Oklahoma, in partnership with ACT, have similar outreach programs to assess and help eighth and ninth graders.

Disadvantaged seventh graders are targeted to receive academic enrichment and mentoring, technology instruction, leadership development and career exploration, summer campus experiences, and an extensive campus visitation program. In Georgia, these experiences are designed to prepare all students to meet the increased college and university admissions standards that are scheduled to go into effect in 2002. Education leaders are also focusing on teacher preparation reform and improved professional development, as well as the alignment of the Hope Scholarship requirements with the new admissions standards. And educators are working to link curricula across all education levels (Crowe, 1998).

Integration of Distance-Learning Efforts

Policymakers and education leaders should take advantage of growing academic offerings available through distance-learning systems as a means to bridge the gap between high school and college.

Kentucky recently created the Virtual High School, which offers advanced math, science, and language courses to high school students statewide. Classes will be offered on-line and supplemented by video and CD-ROM. Certified teachers will provide supportive classroom instruction and grading. Kentucky intends to purchase courses from distance-education companies and institutions in order to prepare students for compliance with new in-state college and university admissions requirements ("Kentucky's New Virtual School," 1999).

Similarly, state community college systems across the nation (Colorado, Pennsylvania, Utah, and California, among others) are establishing electronic community college systems to help meet the needs of adult and place-bound students. State incentives that reward and encourage cooperation and collaboration between state distance-education efforts ultimately will save significant state and institutional resources. Such collaboration helps avoid costly course duplication, while providing another bridge between systems.

State K–16 Councils

States committed to creating more seamless systems should consider establishing K–16 councils or other commissions that have the authority to provide leadership and coordination across sectors in bringing both K–12 and postsecondary education to the table.

Three states—Ohio, Maryland, and Georgia—have undertaken significant statewide K–16 partnerships to focus on education reform. State K–16 councils can function as a communications mechanism for system officials. One repeated strategy across the three states is their creation of common in-state data collection procedures across the K–16 system (Crowe, 1998). Members may include state K–12 and higher education CEOs, business leaders, the governor's office, legislators, education and higher education board members, school and college leaders, parent groups, students, and faculty. Similar councils exist at the local level to ensure that system goals can be adapted to meet the needs of differing areas of the state (Crowe, 1998).

Ohio's K–16 Council created the Ohio Learning Extension Network to link the K–16 community. The network communicates college expectations and defines what entering freshmen should know and be able to do, has developed a continuum of early assessment and intervention services, targets or reallocates existing fiscal resources, and builds a common agenda through a partnership council of state education and higher education board members.

Maryland's K–16 partnership has as its chief goal the development of strategies to strengthen K–16 standards, competencies, assessment systems, and the professional development of teachers, and to promote community involvement in the state's K–16 initiative. The partners hope to create an environment in which there are higher expectations for high school students and changed course-taking behavior, consistent statewide higher education placement standards, improved data collection, and appropriate exit standards in remedial courses.

The long-term goal of the Georgia initiative is to ensure that Georgia students arrive at college fully prepared to succeed academically. The Georgia P–16 initiative seeks to improve student achievement at all levels, facilitate student transitions, ensure that all entering college students are prepared to succeed, improve postsecondary access for minority and low-income students, and focus teacher preparation and professional development programs on meeting high standards for every student.

Federal Policy Support for School-College Collaboration

While education policy is primarily a state and local responsibility, improving access to college is also an important initiative at the U.S. Department of Education. Three federal programs—Tech Prep of the Vocational Education Act, the School-to-Work Opportunities Act, and Goals 2000: Educate America Act—share four policy priorities that support closer school-college collaboration:

- Foster high academic standards and occupational skill development.
- Prepare students well for further education and occupational skill development.
- Support more integration between K–12 and postsecondary institutions.
- Reform public education generally.

A review of the impact of these federal programs (Orr, 2000) identified outcomes and models that have resulted from these federal policy initiatives:

Community colleges in many states have created 2+2 programs leading to associate degree programs in various technical areas.

A community college/K–12 partnership in Florida combined its tech-prep and school-to-work activities to integrate the secondary schools and community colleges in preparing students for advanced technical jobs. The team of K–12, community college, and business partners jointly developed articulated and applied courses that were integrated with work–based learning experiences and provided support for staff development among faculty reaching down as far as middle school.

In North Carolina, a community college and a high school district established a K–14 educational continuum emphasizing high academic standards and technology. Local business leaders worked with the consortium to identify standards for improvement, which led to the establishment of seven new technical programs of study and the revamping of the high school college prep and college-tech prep tracks. Integrated curricula, career development plans, articulation agreements, and industry-sponsored scholarships were all outcomes of the effort.

Governance of these consortia was shared among school district, community college, and other educational and business representatives. Orr (2000) reported other forms of collaboration too:

Awareness activities and information-sharing strategies that involve parents, employers, and educators, some targeted as early as the middle grades, which have the goal of encouraging students to pursue technical careers and a community college education.

Improved preparation for postsecondary technical education. The development of a joint curriculum between community colleges and secondary schools supported a goal of improving teaching and learning.

Student transitions that are simplified by creating structural bridges between community colleges and secondary schools through articulation agreements designed around common course areas and programs of study, by aligning courses, and by encouraging dual enrollment. Comprehensive programs of 2+2 allowed close articulation into community college programs.

All of these strategies contributed to improved student access to the two-year colleges and improved student preparation for college work and for employment. Orr (2000) concludes that the three federal policy initiatives were supportive to varying degrees in establishing an agenda for workforce preparation reform and collaboration between secondary schools and community colleges.

Conclusion

Solutions to these pressing challenges will not be found in policy fiats issued from the state capital. Governors, legislators, and education leaders from K–12, community colleges, and universities must work together to create seamless education systems that support a smooth transition of students from high school to college. It is equally important to involve K–12 teachers, college faculty, and parents as active participants in identifying solutions to these intractable challenges.

Although progress is slow, many states are making progress, and there is much that can be learned from their experience:

State and institutional leaders must think of education as a continuum and work toward removing barriers to student movement between the sectors.

Policymakers should be more consistent and integrated in their own oversight of public and postsecondary education in legislative bodies and other policy forums.

If states want to implement K–16 structures, they need to be willing to reexamine the traditional separation of K–12 and higher education governance. Joint budgeting may be one approach. Another may be commissions that explore specific issues such as admissions and articulation and can help support increased dialogue and communication between sectors.

The challenge for policymakers and education leaders who seek to create seamless systems is twofold: to identify the long- and short-term opportunities and consequences of state intervention and to achieve an appropriate balance between incentives and regulation.

The entire education and state policy community must seriously consider supporting higher academic standards for all high school students, not just those who are in a college-preparatory track. Research shows that a rigorous high school curriculum improves the assessment and placement scores of all students.

In designing accountability systems, state leaders must recognize the connection between high school preparation and outcomes at community colleges and four-year universities.

Policymakers need to create incentives that will encourage cooperation rather than competition among sectors and will provide funding across institutional lines.

State education and policy leaders should continue to support and encourage advanced placement and dual/concurrent enrollment at high schools and community colleges to promote more student transfer and encourage faster time to degree completion.

References

Center for Community College Policy. *State Files History, and Governance of Community Colleges.* [www.communitycollegepolicy.org]. 2000.

Crowe E., *Statewide Remedial Education Policies.* Denver, Colo.: State Higher Education Executive Officers, 1998.

Education Commission of the States. "Transforming Higher Education Requires New Leadership." *State Education Leader,* Spring-Summer 1999, [17(2)].

Education Commission of the States. *State Postsecondary Structures Handbook,* Denver, Colo.: Education Commission of the States, 1997.

Education Commission of the States. *State Policy Issues Affecting School-College Collaboration.* Denver, Colo.: Education Commission of the States, 2000.

Education Reform into the Millennium: The State. "Kentucky's New Virtual School." *University Business,* 1999, 2, 13–14.

Legislature's Role in Building Consensus for Change. Proceedings of a meeting held at Stanford University, Palo Alto, Calif., Sept.-Oct. 1999.

Orr, T., *Community College and Secondary School Collaboration on Workforce Development and Education Reform: A Close Look at Four Community Colleges. Abstract.* New York: Community College Research Center, 2000.

"Reforming Both Houses: Schools and Higher Education." *Thinking K–16.* Education Trust, Fall 1997, 3(1).

Ruppert, S. S., *Transforming Postsecondary Education: Summary of an Invitational ECS Meeting.* Denver: Education Commission of the States, 1999.

Tafel J., and Eberthart, N. *Statewide School-College (K–16) Partnerships to Improve Student Performance.* Denver, Colo.: State Higher Education Executive Officers, 1999.

"Ticket to Nowhere: The Gap Between Leaving High School and Entering College and High Performance Jobs." *Thinking K–16.* Education Trust, Fall 1999, 3(2).

U.S. Department of Education. National Center for Education Statistics. *Remedial Education at Higher Education Institutions in Fall 1995.* by Laurie Lewis and Elizabeth Farris. Bernie Greene, project officer. Washington, DC, 1996.

KATHERINE BOSWELL is the director of the Center for Community College Policy at the Education Commission of the States.

2

*It is not always apparent to K–12 administrators that
collaboration with community colleges will help address
the issues that demand the priority attention of school
leaders.*

A K–12 Perspective on Partnerships
with Community Colleges

Al Azinger

Calls for clearly defined, functional partnerships between postsecondary
institutions and high schools are not new. Attempts to bridge the two sectors were made as early as 1893, when the Committee of Ten standardized
the high school curriculum in response to university concerns about the
uneven academic preparation of graduates from the newly emerging high
schools. More recently, calls for a seamless K–16 curriculum that would blur
distinctions between traditional K–12 schooling and undergraduate education have entered the discussion.

Partnerships between schools and local community colleges have the
potential to constitute an important point of connection between the secondary and postsecondary systems. From the school district's perspective,
these partnerships hold some promise of increasing available resources. For
example, tech-prep programs connect high school students to technical
training facilities and faculty expertise that only the largest districts could
otherwise afford. Similarly, concurrent enrollment programs offer high
school students an opportunity to take honors or advanced placement
courses that would not generate the enrollments needed to justify the allocation of school funds at an individual school level. At a time when school
dollars are spread thin among a wide range of programs designed to meet
growing demands for higher test scores and a well-prepared workforce,
cooperation with community colleges would appear to offer school administrators a valuable resource.

Yet the envisioned seamless working relationships between K–12 districts and community colleges, however desirable, are difficult to achieve.
School superintendents and community college leaders face fundamental

NEW DIRECTIONS FOR COMMUNITY COLLEGES, no. 111, Fall 2000 © Jossey-Bass, a Wiley company

challenges if such a partnership is to work effectively. Some of these challenges emerge from simple yet intractable realities; an example is the physical proximity of schools and community college campuses. Other challenges reflect more complex difficulties posed by the differing professional cultures in which K–12 and community college leaders work.

Proximity

On the less complex side of the spectrum are the logistical challenges that school districts face when attempting to establish workable partnerships with community colleges. Two school districts for which I worked as an administrator illustrate these challenges. Both were of almost identical size, and the socioeconomic distribution among students was comparable. The communities had similar values and expectations of the schools. Each district had a partnership with the nearest community college. But in District A, the neighboring community college had a campus only a few blocks from one high school and was within easy driving distance of the other. In District B, the community college was thirty-five miles from the high school. It was obviously easier for students in District A to get to the community college and take advantage of the courses offered on a dual-enrollment basis. Students did not have to spend a great deal of time away from their friends in high school, and they could return for after-school activities and sports. This was not the case for students in District B. Transportation was arranged, but taking a community college course nonetheless required an afternoon commitment, infringing on students' opportunities to participate in after-school activities.

This situation severely limited the school-community college partnership in District B. There was no lack of goodwill or commitment; cooperation between the school district and the community college was excellent and creative. However, the dual-enrollment programs there never grew because they conflicted with other student needs that have little to do with academics. After a sincere effort at developing a strong partnership with strong curricular content, the number of participating students remained limited. The partnership never dissolved, but it never reached its potential.

Differences in Organizational Culture

Other challenges are much subtler and are embedded in the different cultures of each organization. At the K–12 level, the local school is expected to reflect community values as the designated social institution assigned to help the community raise its children. At a time when the quality of schooling (as reflected in test scores) is under attack, many public schools struggle with the conflict between these values and the state-mandated curricula that stress workforce development. As a result, the high school curriculum tends to be centrally controlled at the district level, and teachers' academic freedom is limited by boundaries established by local boards of education.

While the first community colleges were originally viewed as extensions of the K–12 system, the direction they have taken in the past several decades has resulted in their operational values being shaped by four-year colleges and universities. The result has been a culture that fosters a more open climate to explore controversial topics of study at a level unacceptable in the K–12 system. In addition, the age of the typical community college student allows greater academic and social freedom for both staff and students. Consequently, the nurturing component of schooling that is vital to the K–12 mission is very different at the community college level.

The challenges this presents for smoothly running partnerships between the two institutions manifest themselves in several important ways. Foremost is the custodial nature of K–12 schools. The local school is given the responsibility to ensure the well-being of students assigned to its care. When high schools send their students to the community college, particularly if that college is in another community, it is done with a degree of anxiety regarding the safety and care of the students. K–12 educators need assurances that the community colleges will treat students in a manner that demands responsibility but still recognizes that those students are not adults and therefore carry with them the additional needs that accompany teenagers who are attempting to learn what it means to be an adult. This entails much closer supervision of students (even high school–aged students) than would normally be expected at a community college level. Furthermore, given the highly publicized events of high school violence in the past several years, issues related to student safety have intensified. Instead of looking for ways to increase students' social freedoms during the time students are assigned to the school, administrators are looking for ways to ensure that students are in situations that are safe. The mandate for increased security and safer schools has sometimes been interpreted to mean that the students should stay under closer supervision. School administrators and local school board members may demand what seems to be extraordinary assurance that student safety will be given high consideration.

Another cultural difference emerges in the priorities that guide administrative action. Both community college presidents and K–12 school superintendents work for governing boards that establish policies and articulate the supporting community values that are to guide their respective organizations. But at the K–12 level, the values that have been facing superintendents in recent years focus primarily on school safety and on student achievement as measured by state-mandated assessments. Community colleges, on the other hand, emphasize access to lifelong learning for all local citizens. From the K–12 perspective, therefore, there may be little reason to believe that the community college can support the priority goals that superintendents must address. Indeed, the contemporary push for school-community college partnerships appears to have been driven more by the higher education community than by K–12 leaders. A review of the agenda of the past two annual conferences of the American Association of School Administrators, which represents the nation's school leaders, reveals no sessions devoted to community college partnerships with high schools. A similar review of the past two meetings of the American Association of Community Colleges indicates there were at least eight forums devoted to this topic.

Recommendations

The fact that community college partnerships are not highlighted on the national agenda for superintendents is not to say that the K–12 administrators are uninterested. There have been too many successful collaborations to allow such a conclusion to be drawn. However, it does point out that the rhetoric of the seamless K–16 curriculum should not blind decision makers to the fact that each institution operates in a different political arena with diverse pressures and different constituent groups. It also suggests that if partnerships are to succeed, community college leaders need to be aware of the superintendents' priorities and demonstrate how the community college can help the local district address its needs. Most problems of logistics can eventually be resolved, but they are resolved only if the end result is found to be worth the effort.

Furthermore, if the agenda for increased partnerships is to be advanced, leaders from both institutions must be aware of the diverse needs of the students being targeted and ensure that the programs consider all of those needs. This may mean that the community college will need to think of ways to modify its delivery system to accommodate high school students who place considerable value on being with their contemporaries and participating in school events. A high school principal recently told me that he would gladly send the local community college a good number of students if the college would only schedule the students at a time that worked for the students and the school. Given the evidence suggesting that school-college collaborations are a higher priority for community colleges than for high schools, accommodations of this nature will likely be required if partnerships are to be advanced.

The promise of partnerships does exist. Partnerships do enhance the curriculum for high school students. However, until K–12 educators become convinced that the community college is genuinely interested in helping the local district address those issues that are driving local demands of the school, the concept of partnerships will likely remain only a good idea. In communities where the concept can be translated into a mutually supportive situation in which the urgent agendas of both institutions are given equal consideration, the concept will thrive and students will benefit from the relationship.

AL AZINGER is assistant professor of educational administration and foundations at Illinois State University. Previously he was superintendent of schools in Lawrence, Kansas.

3

Far from perfect, the value of tech prep thus far is its contribution as a test bed of ideas associated with secondary-to-postsecondary transition.

Maximizing the Benefits of Tech-Prep Initiatives for High School Students

Debra D. Bragg

Although tech prep is not entirely new, it is a relative newcomer to the nation's educational reform agenda. Certainly it is unique in its emphasis on preparing students who might otherwise not have considered postsecondary education for the transition to the community college. With more students than ever before continuing their education at community colleges (Boesel and Fredland, 1999), it is important to examine how tech prep is progressing and whether it is indeed helping more students to make the transition from high school to college. Understanding lessons about how tech prep works most successfully may help to inform future K–16 collaborative endeavors, particularly those focused on assisting youths to make successful transitions to community colleges.

Progress on Tech-Prep Implementation

Tech prep was launched nationwide in 1991 and 1992, several years after the idea was conceived by Dale Parnell in his book *The Neglected Majority* (1985). Overshadowed at the time by *A Nation at Risk* (National Commission on Excellence in Education, 1983), with its accent on traditional academics, tech prep did not draw attention until the federal Carl D. Perkins Vocational and Applied Technology Act Amendments of 1990 (commonly known as Perkins II) authorized the Tech Prep Education Act, targeting federal funding toward the implementation of 2+2 programs. Soon after, in 1994, the School-to-Work Opportunities Act (STWOA) was passed, reinforcing the tech-prep model and advancing the notion of secondary-to-postsecondary articulation as part of more broadly reformed educational systems for all students. STWOA emphasized combining school and work in more creative and challenging ways for all students. Still later, under the most recent version of the Carl D. Perkins federal legislation (referred to as Perkins III), passed in 1998, the conception of tech prep was expanded to include the baccalaureate, providing tech-prep consortia with the option of creating bachelor's-level capstone programs for two-year degrees.

Among a multitude of goals, tech prep was intended to establish formal articulation agreements identifying rigorous academic and technical programs of study having a logical progression from the secondary to the postsecondary level. Through at least a 2+2 sequential curriculum, tech prep was seen as an avenue for students who might not normally consider college to pursue careers requiring postsecondary-level math, science, and technology. By engaging high school students in learning for and about technologically focused career pathways, tech prep could prepare students to complete college credentials and technical careers. Along with curriculum (academic and technical) integration, closer alliances between school- and work-based learning, workplace mentoring, and career guidance and exploration became valued elements of tech prep in some communities, building on notions advanced by STWOA.

Although tech prep started out to respond to the needs of a specific group (students between the twenty-fifth and seventy-fifth percentile of high school class rank or other measures of academic performance), some educators have come to see tech prep as an avenue for systemic reform (see, for example, Gray and Herr, 1995; Hull and Grevelle, 1998). From this perspective, tech prep is an educational policy focused on what McDonnell and Elmore (1987) consider capacity building because it is geared toward improving the educational system overall. Increasingly reflecting this expanded vision, by 1995, with just three to four years of implementation in most localities, tech prep existed in some capacity in "almost 70 percent of U.S. school districts serving 88 percent of all American high school students" (Hershey, Silverberg, Owens, and Hulsey, 1998, p. 22).

As of yet little is known about how tech prep affects student outcomes, and this is a serious concern. However, it is difficult to evaluate student outcomes before an educational initiative has been fully implemented and institutionalized. Only recently have tech-prep programs that started in the early 1990s reached a point where high school participants have graduated from high school and made the transition to college or work. Understanding this context, in January 1998 Bragg and others (1999) launched a longitudinal investigation of tech-prep participants in eight regions of the United States. Preliminary results after two years of this four-year longitudinal study show that the majority of tech-prep participants have engaged in substantial academic and technical course work at the secondary level and moved on to two-year or four-year college at very high rates. Across all eight consortia, at least 70 percent of tech-prep participants have entered a postsecondary institution within one to three years of high school graduation. Most went to a community college directly out of high school, and many of these students also held part-time jobs related to their studies. Bragg and colleagues are conducting additional work to determine the academic performance, persistence, and credentialing of these tech-prep participants through the fall semester of 2000.

In addition to this longitudinal analysis, national studies of implementation policies and practices show advances over time (Boesel, Rahn, and Deich, 1994; Bragg, Layton, and Hammons, 1994; Bragg and others, 1997; Hershey, Silverberg, and Owens, 1995; Hershey, Silverberg, Owens, and Hulsey, 1998). Benefits of tech prep have included stronger linkages between high schools, colleges (mostly two-year), and employers. Enhanced partnerships between organizations have been created when more collaboration has occurred among people, especially academic and technical instructors and educators and business representatives. Tech prep has encouraged professional development and curriculum development as vehicles for bringing people together, sometimes yielding greater awareness of the challenges that students face when moving from high school into college or the workplace. It also has encouraged faculty to change instructional practices, including more emphasis on linking theory to practice and enhanced use of real-world contexts for learning traditional academic subject matter. At the same time, tech-prep initiatives have emphasized that students who are sometimes thought of as noncollege bound should participate in more rigorous math and science instruction rather than lower-level academics. Tech prep has also encouraged work-based learning to assist students to explore a broad range of related occupational clusters designed to help them sort out future education and career goals, rather than specific skills training for immediate job placement after high school.

No change is simple, and results from national implementation studies reveal pervasive barriers to tech prep. Nationwide consortia struggle to find time for instructors to meet and plan jointly for integrated academic and technical curriculum, articulation agreements, dual-credit courses, and the like. Moreover, confusion about the purpose of tech prep and whether it is a continuation of failed educational approaches of the past has created tremendous barriers to faculty participation. Although many community colleges have played a supportive role, few have accepted far-reaching goals that are needed to create sequential, articulated curricular restructuring across the secondary and postsecondary levels. Many community colleges appear satisfied to receive the products (that is, the students) of high schools without committing to the foundational curriculum work needed to make tech prep successful. At the postsecondary level, changes to instructional pedagogy, academic standards, and articulation of two-year degrees with four-year degrees have been slow to evolve. No doubt some of this lack of attention to tech prep by community college officials has been due to the concentration of fiscal resources at the secondary level. Tech prep cannot become fully implemented without recreating an entire sequence of secondary and postsecondary curriculum, requiring more equitable distribution of resources across levels.

Reviewing these findings, it seems clear that tech-prep implementation continues to evolve slowly due to the constraints created by the existing K–16 system. Still, tech prep has had some initial successes, and these can be attributed in large part to better collaborative processes between high schools and community colleges. By examining key features of collaborative tech-prep initiatives, valuable insights can be identified for future secondary-to-postsecondary partnerships.

Features of Successful Tech-Prep Programs

To varying degrees, tech-prep initiatives have core components geared toward enhancing students' opportunities to make a successful transition from high school to community college and work, sometimes also including transition to four-year college. Studies of tech-prep implementation repeatedly point to components that can serve as guideposts for successful programming.

Bragg (1995) noted six core components that remain evident in successful tech-prep initiatives today: formal articulation strategies, rigorous and engaging learning, meaningful linkages between theory and practice, outcomes-focused curriculum, access and opportunity for all, and longevity through collaboration. Although they emerged from tech-prep initiatives, these six components could underpin nearly any secondary-to-postsecondary transition system.

Formal Articulation Strategies. Formal articulation can draw more high school students into college by putting into writing a well-planned, sequential course of study that provides a logical pathway of courses from high school to college attainment. Although many tech-prep participants have failed to cash in on articulated credits (Dornsife, 1997), some consortia have implemented articulation agreements successfully. For example, in Victoria, Texas, over one-quarter of all graduates of the twenty high schools feeding into Victoria College have participated in articulated courses in recent years, and a large proportion of these students have earned dual credits. At the Miami Valley Tech Prep Consortium in Dayton, Ohio, tenth-grade students are given the same academic placement exams as new entrants to Sinclair Community College. Armed with knowledge of how they would place if they made the transition to college right away, tenth-grade students learn why they need to take rigorous courses at the high school level.

The Miami Valley Tech Prep consortium provides another incentive to encourage high school students to enroll at Sinclair. Upon high school graduation, tech-prep participants are eligible for a college scholarship guaranteeing free or minimal tuition if they continue full time in tech prep. For students who would forego college because of financial concerns, this scholarship provides a powerful incentive to advance to college.

Rigorous and Engaging Learning. This is essential if high school students are going to be prepared to matriculate in college successfully. No doubt student transition is enhanced when learning in grades K–12 is rigorous and carefully linked to postsecondary learning. Educational experiences that are integrated, student focused, and project based can be highly motivating, encouraging youths to remain connected to the learning process over time (Resnick, 1987; Rosenstock, 1991). Such goals are evident at the New York City Technical College, where high school seniors are encouraged to participate in a college-level interdisciplinary transition course that also satisfies a high school English credit known as, of all things, "Great Thinkers in Science." Among several "Great Thinkers" courses that have sprung up in recent years, "Great Thinkers in Science" integrates math, science, and technology in an exploration of Galileo, Kepler, Darwin, Freud, and Edison (Frenkel and Gawkins, 1995).

In another case, the Mt. Hood Education Partnership in Gresham, Oregon, has developed a sequential curriculum based on outcomes, in addition to curriculum guides and course syllabi. At the secondary level, core curriculum centers on academic (math, science, English) competencies that are intimately connected to broad career pathways. At the postsecondary level, the focus on technical instruction and career preparation increases, but not without the support of integrated academic content.

Meaningful Linkages of Theory to Practice. These are emphasized to link learning in the school setting to the genuine laboratory of the workplace and community, enhancing the secondary-to-postsecondary transition process further. Many educators who implement tech prep believe the gulf between theory and practice is problematic. To counter this concern, tech prep connects the theory and practice inherent in academic and technical education. In fact, in the Perkins III legislation, work-based learning is an explicit goal of tech prep. One purpose of this alternative approach to instruction is to provide students with a greater understanding of how academic and technical content is integrated in modern-day work.

Both Danville Area Community College (Illinois) and Guilford Technical Community College (North Carolina) use a combined tech-prep and youth apprenticeship approach and encourage students to pursue intensive work-based learning opportunities in such career fields as manufacturing, accounting, banking, and various health occupations. School-to-college matriculation rates are very high for students in these programs. For example, in Danville, 95 percent of high school youth apprentices have continued on to Danville Area Community College, and many of these students plan to continue to the baccalaureate level (Bragg and others, 1999).

Outcomes-Focused Curriculum. An emphasis on outcomes establishes clear goals for student performance throughout the secondary-to-postsecondary transition process. Identifying outcomes linked to academic and technical standards helps to ensure that graduates acquire the competencies needed to attain their desired goals, including immediate employment or enrollment in further education. In addition to state-level standards that are being implemented nationwide, the Secretary's Commission on Achieving Necessary Skills (1991), Goals 2000, and the occupational credentials advocated by the STWOA all reinforce the importance of outcomes-based curriculum (Orr, 1998). Bailey and Merritt (1997) point out that a growing number of selective colleges are recognizing the merits of students having interests and commitments outside of school. By using alternative or authentic forms of assessment such as portfolios, projects, or performance-based assessments, students can demonstrate their knowledge and skills in a realistic manner (Murnane and Levy, 1996; Resnick and Wirt, 1996). States such as Maryland, Oregon, and Wisconsin are experimenting with new forms of assessment for college admissions, using alternative approaches to document the competencies of learners in programs such as tech prep and reducing barriers that once precluded these students from entrance into college.

Access and Opportunity for All Students. Emphasizing access and opportunity for all is an important component that represents a difference between where the notion of tech prep started (Parnell, 1985) and where it is today. Since passage of the federal STWOA legislation and increased understanding of the problems created when students are segregated from their peers (potentially perpetuating tracking), tech prep has changed in many localities. More educators now describe tech prep as appropriate for students who appear at every point on the academic ability continuum (Bragg and others, 1997), deliberately steering away from the creation of specific courses that could label students or possibly limit their options for more advanced academic studies. Increasingly educators are infusing contextual learning principles into all academic courses and career-technical ones as well.

In Hillsborough County, Florida, college tech-prep enrollments are growing because of the advantages this model affords students preparing to matriculate from high school to either a community college or four-year college or university. Evaluation results obtained by Bragg and others (1999) show that while over half of high school graduates who have participated in tech prep in high school have continued on to Hillsborough Community College, the transition to four-year college is also substantial. One-third of Hillsborough's tech-prep graduates go on to four-year colleges immediately after high school graduation.

Collaboration at All Levels. Collaboration between educational sectors is critical if the goal of enhancing student learning is central to successful student transition from school to college or work. Joint planning between the secondary and postsecondary levels and between academic and career-technical educators is essential to overcoming turf battles.

To help overcome barriers to joint planning, Volunteer State Community College in Nashville, Tennessee, has offered professional development for faculty from both the secondary and postsecondary levels, mostly to enhance communication and break down barriers. Similarly, in the CREATE partnership in Oklahoma City, faculty who engage in collaborative endeavors are rewarded with special opportunities to attend workshops and conferences. Potential problems over control of curriculum and distribution of resources are resolved when people talk to one another and recognize that they contribute to a common goal: to assist students in making a successful transition. Based on her research in four states (Florida, Pennsylvania, New Jersey, and North Carolina), Orr (1998) has shown that the more that boundaries, goals, and practices mesh between existing secondary and post-secondary levels, the more effective new transition systems can be. Whether simple or complex, the most effective governance systems involve a wide range of community groups in significant ways (Hershey, Silverberg, and Owens, 1995). Without broad representation, there is less chance that students—particularly students least likely to see themselves as college bound—will succeed in the transition process.

Conclusion

Historians Tyack and Cuban (1995) argue that reforming education is complex because it challenges deeply held beliefs about what "real school" is all about. To make sustained improvements, they believe there must be a commitment to improving all of education—not just "tinkering with reform." As an emerging school-to-college and -work vehicle, tech prep offers valuable lessons to help educators design new transition systems that provide opportunities for more students to go to college. Much more investigation is needed to understand how tech-prep implementation processes are linked to student outcomes. Still, preliminary studies yield encouraging results regarding student transition to college. Far from perfect, tech prep has been valuable as a test bed of ideas associated with secondary-to-postsecondary transition. In many communities, tech prep is making progress, and the lessons it offers can contribute to building even stronger relationships between high schools and community colleges in the future.

References

Bailey, T., and Merritt, D. *School-to-Work for the College Bound.* Berkeley: National Center for Research in Vocational Education, University of California, Berkeley, 1997.

Boesel, D., and Fredland, E. *College for All.* Washington, D.C.: U.S. Department of Education, National Library of Education, Office of Educational Research and Improvement, 1999.

Boesel, D., Rahn, M., and Deich, S. *National Assessment of Vocational Education, Final Report to Congress.* Vol. 2: *Program Improvement: Education Reform.* Washington, D.C.: U.S. Department of Education, Office of Educational Research and Improvement, 1994.

Bragg, D. "Linking High Schools to Postsecondary Institutions: The Role of Tech Prep." In W. N. Grubb (ed.), *Education Through Occupations in American High Schools.* New York: Teachers College Press, 1995.

Bragg, D., Layton, J., and Hammons, F. *Tech Prep Implementation in the United States: Promising Trends and Lingering Challenges.* Berkeley: National Center for Research in Vocational Education, University of California, Berkeley, 1994.

Bragg, D. D., and others. *Tech Prep/School to Work Partnerships: More Trends and Challenges.* Berkeley: National Center for Research in Vocational Education, University of California at Berkeley, 1997.

Bragg, D. D., and others. *Tech Prep Implementation and Preliminary Outcomes for Eight Local Tech Prep Consortia.* Berkeley: National Center for Research in Vocational Education, University of California at Berkeley, 1999.

Dornsife, C. "The Postsecondary Partner." In E. N. Andrew and others (eds.), *Lessons Learned: Five Years in the Urban Schools Network.* Berkeley: National Center for Research in Vocational Education, University of California, Berkeley, 1997.

Frenkel, M., and Gawkins, A. "The Missing Link." *Vocational Education Journal,* 1995, 70(4), 26–27, 43.

Gray, K. C., and Herr, E. L. *Other Ways to Win: Creating Alternatives for High School Graduates.* Thousand Oaks, Calif.: Corwin Press, 1995.

Hershey, A., Silverberg, M., and Owens, T. *The Diverse Forms of Tech Prep: Implementation Approaches in Ten Local Consortia.* Princeton, N.J.: Mathematica Policy Research, 1995.

Hershey, A. M., Silverberg, M. K., Owens, T., and Hulsey, L. K. *Focus for the Future: The Final Report of the National Tech-Prep Evaluation.* Princeton, N.J.: Mathematica Policy Research, 1998.

Hull, D., and Grevelle, J. *Tech Prep: The Next Generation.* Waco, Tex.: Next Generation, 1998.

McDonnell, L. M., and Elmore, R. F. "Getting the Job Done: Alternative Policy Instruments." *Educational Evaluation and Policy Analysis,* 1987, 9(2), 133–152.

Murnane, R. J., and Levy, F. *Teaching and New Basic Skills.* New York: Free Press, 1996.

National Commission on Excellence in Education. *A Nation at Risk: The Imperative for Educational Reform.* Washington, D.C.: National Commission on Excellence in Education, 1983.

Orr, M. T. "Integrating Secondary Schools and Community Colleges Through School-to-Work Transition and Educational Reform." *Journal of Vocational Education Research,* 1998, 23(1), 93–111.

Parnell, D. (1985). *The Neglected Majority.* Washington, D.C.: American Association of Community Colleges, 1985.

Resnick, L. B. (1987). "Learning in School and Out." *Educational Research, 16,* 13–20.

Resnick, L. B., and Wirt, J. *Linking School and Work: Roles for Standards and Assessment.* San Francisco: Jossey-Bass, 1996.

Rosenstock, L. "The Walls Come Down: The Overdue Reunification of Vocational and Academic Education." *Phi Delta Kappan,* 1991, 72(6), 434–435.

Secretary's Commission on Achieving Necessary Skills. *What Work Requires of Schools: A SCANS Report for America 2000.*

Tyack, D., and Cuban, L. *Tinkering Toward Utopia: A Century of Public School Reform.* Cambridge, Ma.: Harvard University Press, 1995.

Washington, D.C.: U.S. Department of Labor, 1991.

Washington, D.C.: U.S. Department of Education, 1998.

DEBRA D. BRAGG *is associate professor of community college leadership at the University of Illinois at Urbana-Champaign.*

4

Secondary school juniors and seniors no longer should find it convenient to "blow off the senior year" or part of the junior year as well. Dual-credit programs, carried out largely by community and technical colleges, have opened the door to thousands of secondary school honor students and vocationally oriented students who need to stay challenged as they complete high school.

Lessons Learned from Current State and National Dual-Credit Programs

Hans A. Andrews

During the mid-1980s, while I was the dean of instruction at a community college in central Illinois, administrators from a neighboring parochial school asked if we would consider offering college courses for juniors and seniors at their school during the school day. They were concerned that far too many of their very best students were "blowing off" their senior year, marking time until graduation by opting for soft electives rather than enrolling in challenging academic courses. Many had completed the courses required for college entrance and had no incentives to take difficult classes.

The college responded by offering classes that met the curricular requirements of both institutions. The high school's curriculum, based on the "James Madison High School" program outlined by Bennett (1987), included a twelve-unit segment (25 percent of the college-prep track) that could be customized to meet unique school needs. This open portion of the curriculum could quite logically be filled by the college courses. At the same time, care was taken to ensure the collegiate integrity of the courses. The community college guaranteed that the courses were transferable to four-year institutions in Illinois, the majority of the faculty members teaching the courses would come from the full-time ranks, and all faculty members teaching the courses would be highly qualified in their respective subject areas. Because the courses met the needs of both school and college, students could use them to earn both high school credit and advanced placement credit, which could be applied to the college of their choice.

This is just one example of how community colleges help high school students get a head start on college and make the most of their senior year,

New Directions for Community Colleges, no. 111, Fall 2000 © Jossey-Bass, a Wiley company

which all too often leaves students in a meaningless holding pattern until graduation (Marshall and Andrews, 1991; Kronholz, 1999).

Trends in Dual-Credit Enrollment

National data on the number of high school students participating in dual-enrollment programs are not routinely collected. Yet there is some evidence that dual enrollment is on the rise. For example, the National Center for Education Statistics (1997, 1999) reports that the number of students under the age of eighteen who enrolled in public two-year colleges on a part-time basis increased from 96,913 in the fall of 1993 to 123,039 in the fall of 1995. This group of part-timers, which probably accounts for most students in dual-enrollment programs, rose as a proportion of all part-time community college students from 2.8 percent in 1993 to 3.6 percent in 1995.

Stronger evidence of potential growth can be seen in the many state initiatives that have encouraged dual enrollment. For example, Minnesota lawmakers enacted legislation in 1985 that enables high-achieving secondary school students to take courses at the community colleges, state universities, the University of Minnesota, and other higher education institutions (Gerber, 1987). The number of participating high school students rose from 3,528 (3 percent of all eligible juniors and seniors) in 1985–86 to 6,671 (6 percent of all eligible juniors and seniors) in 1994–95 (Minnesota Office of the Legislative Auditor, 1996). Almost half (45 percent) of the students participating in 1994–95 took community college courses, and an additional 18 percent enrolled in classes that technical colleges offered (Minnesota Office of the Legislative Auditor, 1996).

Washington and Florida provide additional data. Washington's Running Start program began in 1990 as a pilot project involving five colleges. It expanded to statewide operation in 1992–93, enrolling approximately 3,350 high school students in community college classes. The Washington State Board for Community and Technical Colleges (1999) reports that the number of enrollees increased to 12,355 students in 1998–99. In Florida, state statute (Florida Statutes, section 240.116[1]) requires school superintendents and community college presidents to implement an articulation agreement that, among other things, specifies the following: courses and programs for dual enrollment, eligibility requirements for student participation in dual-enrollment opportunities, "institutional responsibilities regarding student screening prior to enrollment and monitoring student performance," criteria for judging the quality of dual-enrollment courses, "institutional responsibilities for assuming the cost of dual enrollment courses," and mechanisms for "converting college credit hours earned through dual enrollment and early admission programs to high school credit based on mastery of course outcomes." Windham (1997) reports that the number of high school students taking community college classes under these dual-enrollment provisions rose from 19,375 in 1992 to 46,541 in 1996–97.

Several other states have similar laws. For example, Missouri legislation, first passed in 1990 and then amended in 1999, stipulates that "public high schools may, in cooperation with Missouri public community colleges and public or private four-year colleges and universities, offer postsecondary course options to high school students" (Missouri Revised Statutes, section 167.223). For the purposes of state aid, students are counted both within the average daily attendance reports of the school districts and as resident students at the community colleges. New Mexico passed similar legislation in 1990, allowing dual reimbursement to both schools and the community colleges, as did Illinois in 1997 (New Mexico Association of Community Colleges, 1990; Illinois Community College Board, 1999). These dual-payment options should lead to an explosion in dual-credit secondary school enrollments in the years to come. Administrators and governing boards will no longer have to be concerned about how much income the program is taking away from the secondary schools.

Other states seek efficiencies by eliminating overlap between the curricula at high schools and colleges. Massachusetts specifies that dual-enrollment courses should be those that the high schools themselves do not offer; eligible students are those who have a grade point average of 3.0 or above and have a demonstrated ability to benefit from college-level work (Massachusetts Department of Education, 1999). Similarly, Michigan's Postsecondary Enrollment Options Act authorizes high school students to enroll in college courses only if those courses are not offered by the school district or if they are not available to students because of scheduling conflicts (Michigan Department of Education, 1999). The school districts themselves are responsible for tuition and fees with state school aid funds; cash payment to both the school district and the college is not part of the Michigan policy at this time. Furthermore, dual-enrollment opportunities are limited to juniors and seniors who have achieved specified academic standards as measured by the state's high school proficiency tests.

The Quality Factor

The movement of colleges into dual-enrollment programs has occasioned concern for the academic rigor of the classes offered in these programs. Lambert and Mercurio (1986, p. 28) clearly stated this in the mid-1980s, when policymakers in Missouri were first considering policy options for dual-enrollment offerings:

> Currently there are no explicitly defined criteria to help distinguish programs that are well-administered from those that may be haphazard. Thus, as high school-college cooperative programs proliferate, college deans, admissions officers, registrars and faculty advisers face the problem of evaluating fairly the college credits earned by high school students. They must decide whether

to award students academic credit, exempt students from required courses, place students in advanced courses, or give students no recognition whatsoever.

States have responded to these concerns in a variety of ways, stipulating the conditions under which dual-enrollment classes will be delivered. Emphasis has been placed on ensuring that students are eligible for college-level work, that the instructors teaching dual-credit courses are qualified to teach at the college level, and that college credit that students earn in dual-enrollment courses can be transferred to baccalaureate-granting institutions.

Missouri. The Missouri Coordinating Board for Higher Education (CBHE) established "principles of good practice" for dual-credit programs, requiring colleges to articulate "clear and uniform expectations relative to (1) student eligibility, (2) program structure and administration, (3) faculty qualifications and support, (4) assessment of student performance, and (5) transferability of credit." In addition, responsibility for course quality was assigned to college academic departments. This stipulation gave full-time faculty members a key role in the design and delivery of courses. Faculty responsibilities include approving the appointment of instructors teaching dual-credit courses and helping in the development of course assessment and evaluation measures.

The Missouri CBHE plans to keep an updated list of the dual-credit programs that comply with the board's policy. This list does not constitute a legal endorsement, nor does it constitute a form of informal accreditation. But it does alert school districts, as consumers, about the relative quality and transferability of college-level, dual-enrollment courses available to their students (Girardi and Stein, 1999, p. 17).

Illinois. The Illinois Community College Board (ICCB) (1999, p. 63) specifies that instructors in the dual-credit courses "shall be selected, employed and evaluated by the community college, selected from full-time faculty and/or from adjunct faculty with appropriate credentials and demonstrated teaching competencies at the college level." In addition, the students are to have appropriate qualifications, a high level of motivation, and adequate time to devote to college-level work. The ICCB also asks for students to be able to satisfy course placement tests or other course prerequisites so that they will have the same qualifications and assurance of preparation as the other college students have.

Virginia. Carr (1997) reports that "equivalency is necessary if students who transfer to four-year institutions are to receive credit for dual-credit instruction, thus enabling them to complete baccalaureate degrees without taking additional credits" (p. 1) The state's "Categories of Good Practices" list the following as assurances that help guarantee the quality of dual-credit programs: course equivalency, student readiness and eligibility, student placement, and faculty qualifications and evaluation. The Virginia system also encourages full-time faculty members and division chairs to observe and evaluate instructors who are teaching dual-credit classes.

North Dakota. Policy in this state stipulates that dual-credit courses must meet the content and academic standards of the course sections taught on the campuses. The state's policy also makes very clear that "the dual-credit course taught in the high school is a college course which offers high school credit and NOT a high school course which receives college credit" (North Dakota University System, 1999, p. 3).

Florida. Legislation in Florida spells out the qualifications of those who teach in the state's Articulated Acceleration program: "Faculty, community college and high school, teaching credit courses in the following areas: humanities/fine arts; social/behavioral sciences; and natural sciences/mathematics; must have completed at least 18 graduate semester hours in the teaching discipline and hold at least a master's degree, or hold the minimum of a master's degree with a major in the teaching discipline."

Course Delivery

Besides attending to the issue of course quality, administrators who oversee dual-enrollment programs must consider course delivery options. Experience across the states is varied. In Minnesota, students go to the campuses during the day to enroll in on-campus course sections (Gerber, 1987). Massachusetts limits dual enrollment to courses that are taught on the main campus of the college offering the class; courses taught on satellite campuses or by distance-learning technologies are not eligible (Massachusetts Department of Education, 1999).

Some states leave decisions about course delivery to the individual colleges. Michigan, for example, allows students to elect college courses during the school day, evening, or weekend; and on-campus, off-campus, or through interactive television (Michigan Department of Education, 1999). Illinois is another state that offers few limitations. Mees (1999) found that of the dual-enrollment classes offered by the state's community colleges, 24 percent were offered on-campus, 17 percent were offered at off-campus locations (excluding high schools), 27 percent were offered in the high schools themselves, 13 percent held in distance-learning classrooms, and 10 percent were offered through interactive TV.

Implications for College Administrators

Dual-credit programs are one of the most meaningful ways that community colleges and secondary schools can build strong relationships. State policies, driven by legislators' interest in shortening the time it takes to complete an associate or bachelor's degree, can further these dual-enrollment opportunities.

Secondary schools within states that do not deduct funds for students enrolled in collegiate dual-credit courses have proven to be much more supportive of encouraging qualified students to enroll. A recent unpublished survey of Illinois community colleges provides corroborating evidence. All forty-eight colleges responding to the survey indicated yes to the question, "Has the dual-credit program at your college increased since the state started allowing funding for both the secondary schools and the colleges?" (Andrews, 2000).

Working with schools in the establishment of dual-credit opportunities for students, however, needs to be handled with a great deal of sensitivity. Not all secondary school teachers are going to rally in support of this concept. They will have fears of losing classes of exceptional students whom they might otherwise be assigned to teach. Community college faculty members, for their part, will have concerns about going down to the secondary school to teach high school students. These fears and concerns must be dealt with as a potential relationship between the college and high school evolves.

Strong leadership by administration and enlightened faculty will do much to minimize these concerns. Good faculty in secondary schools will find they have a new challenge. They will now be expected to prepare their best students to take college-level classes as juniors and seniors. They will also be able to take much pride in seeing these students enrolling in these programs. College faculty will discover early on that they may have their best class of the semester at the secondary school. All students in an English or psychology class, for example, will be honor students.

Parents of secondary school students are a key element to include in the planning process. A good orientation program for students and their parents on what dual-credit means and how it works for the benefit of a son or daughter is extremely important. Parents will need to know, and will gain much pride from the fact, that their children are selected for this important program. They will be highly motivated to support the programs when they understand that their child may be able to achieve one semester or one year of college credit while still completing high school requirements.

John Cavan, president of Southside Virginia Community College (SVCC), shared an example of such a success story with me. One of the college's dual-credit students was accepted for transfer into the College of William and Mary and then into Harvard graduate school. The student, who had completed most of his general requirements through SVCC, ended up at the top of his college graduating class of 1,119 students (Hales, 1997).

The quality of the instructors cannot be overemphasized. Dual-credit courses put the reputation of the college on the line among the high school faculty and the students who enroll. If an average or weak instructor is selected from the college to teach the course, the feedback to high school teachers will be immediate. Over the years I have heard students say to their high school teachers, "The college teacher is easier than you are." If the instructor is selected from the high school to teach the dual-credit course, it is just as important that this instructor be highly respected, qualified, and have similar credentials as the college faculty members on campus who do the teaching. These high school faculty members are often already teaching at the college on a part-time basis in the evenings or weekends. Mentoring and orientation to the college syllabus are vital for high school faculty who work on dual-credit offerings.

The enrollment of students, midterm and final grade reporting, and other support services should be as much in line with what the college provides other students as possible. Pretesting helps students realize the importance of good effort in high school courses leading up to the dual-credit offerings. Some students will not make that effort but must be led to understand that another semester or year of good study in the high school courses should get them ready for the following semester or year of dual-credit offerings. Some of these concerns are not as prevalent in states where dual-credit courses are taken only at the college setting. It is much more important to articulate and communicate well with the secondary personnel when the courses are offered in the high school.

One of the concerns that college faculty expressed to me when we were starting dual-credit classes is that we will not get those students to take our classes on campus. Experience has shown that the opposite is true. Some of the dual-credit students realize that the quality of their classes is high and may enroll for one or more years at the same community college where they took dual-credit courses. The parochial school in Northern Illinois that we worked with increased enrollment of its graduates from thirteen to fourteen freshmen a year to forty to forty-five at the college. The stigma of enrolling in a community college rather than a university often disappears or is of minimal concern once the college proves itself through the continued success of the dual-credit students.

Another potential concern lies in the question of whether the college, which serves large numbers of adult part-time students, is prepared to respond to the needs of younger school-age students. In the dual-enrollment programs I have administered at two community colleges, I have never found this to be a problem. Not once has immaturity or lack of readiness for college-level material posed significant problems for the faculty members in teaching dual-enrollment programs. Although my perspective may be limited, I believe it is supported by the continued success of advanced placement programs in secondary schools throughout the United States.

Conclusion

By focusing on the sensitivities of students, faculty, and administrators at both the secondary school and community college levels, a meaningful dual-credit program can emerge and help hundreds of secondary school students stay challenged and get ahead in their college work.

References

Andrews, H. A. *The Dual-Credit Explosion in Illinois Community Colleges.* Olney, Ill.: Olney Central College, Summer 2000.

Bennett, W. J. *James Madison High School: A Curriculum for American Students.* Washington, D.C.: U. S. Department of Education, 1987.

Carr, L.L. *Principles of Good Practice for Dual-Credit Programs.* Richmond, Va.: Virginia Community College, 1997.

Florida State Board of Community Colleges. *High School and Community College Dual Enrollment: Issues of Rigor and Transferability.* Tallahassee: Florida State Board of Community Colleges, 1997.

Gerber, C. *High School/College Brief.* Supplement to *AACJC Letter,* May 19, 1987.

Girardi, A. G., and Stein, R. B. *State Dual Credit Policy and Its Implications for Community Colleges: Lessons from Missouri for the 21st Century.* Jefferson City, Mo.: Missouri Coordinating Board for Higher Education, 1999.

Hales, C. "Harvard Grad Student Attended SVCC Dual Program." *SVCC Connections Newsletter,* 1997, *1*(4).

Illinois Community College Board. *Administrative Rules of the Illinois Community College Board.* Springfield: Illinois Community College Board, 1999.

Kronholz, J. "Academic Question: Why Has Senior Year of High School Lost Its Purpose for Many?" *Wall Street Journal,* Mar. 23, 1999, p. 83.

Lambert, L. M., and Mercurio, J. A. "Making Decisions: College Credits Earned in High School." *Journal of College Admissions,* 1986, no. 111, 28–32.

Marshall, R. P., and Andrews, H. A. "Challenging High School Honor Students with Community College Courses." *Community College Review,* 1991, *19*(1), 47–51.

Massachusetts Department of Education. *The Massachusetts Dual Enrollment Program.* Malden, Mass.: Massachusetts Department of Education, 1999. [http://www.doe.mass.edu/doedocs/news/cm497bro.html].

Mees, R. *Dual Credit Courses: Survey Information from Selected Community Colleges in Illinois.* Carterville, Ill.: John A. Logan College, 1999.

Michigan Department of Education. *Postsecondary Enrollment Options Act Update for Fall of 1999.* Lansing, Mich.: Michigan Department of Education, 1999. [http://cdp.mde.state.mi.us/TalentDevelopment/PSEO/Update99.html].

Minnesota Office of the Legislative Auditor. *Postsecondary Enrollment Options Program.* St. Paul: Minnesota Office of the Legislative Auditor, 1996. [http://www.auditor.leg.state.mn.us/ped/pedrep/9605ful.pdf].

National Center for Education Statistics. *Digest of Education Statistics, 1996.* Washington, D.C.: U.S. Department of Education, 1997. [http://www.nces.ed.gov/pubsearch/pubsinfo.asp?pubid=96133].

National Center for Education Statistics. *Digest of Education Statistics, 1998.* Washington, D.C.: U.S. Department of Education, 1999. [http://www.nces.ed.gov/pubs99/digest98/d98t176.html].

New Mexico Association of Community Colleges. *New Mexico Policies Governing Concurrent Enrollment of Secondary Students at Postsecondary Institutions.* Santa Fe: New Mexico Association of Community Colleges, 1990.

North Dakota University System. *The Delivery of Dual-Credit College Courses by the North Dakota University System. Academic Affairs Council Guidelines.* Bismarck, N.D.: North Dakota University System, 1999.

Washington State Board for Community and Technical Colleges. *Running Start, 1998–99 Annual Progress Report.* Olympia: Washington State Board for Community and Technical Colleges, 1999. [http://www.sbctc.ctc.edu/Pub/runstart_989.pdf].

Windham, P. *Dual Enrollment Is Alive and Well in Florida's Community College System.* Tallahassee: State Board of Community Colleges, 1997. [http://www.dcc.firn.edu/dccrepts/oeer/ff02.htm].

HANS A. ANDREWS is president of Olney Central College, Illinois.

5

Since 1973, middle college high schools, sponsored by local community colleges, have worked with local school districts as well as parents to create unique learning environments for at-risk youth. This chapter provides a model for the planning and operation of a new institution based on Middle College at LaGuardia Community College (New York) and Mott Middle College at Mott Community College (Michigan).

Establishing and Sustaining a Middle College High School

Cecilia L. Cunningham, Chery S. Wagonlander

Over the past twenty-five years, more than twenty-five high school-college collaborations have been created and have thrived as middle colleges. These programs are direct spin-offs from Middle College High School, which opened in 1973 at LaGuardia Community College in New York. The design for the middle college concept evolved from the work of Janet Lieberman, professor of psychology at LaGuardia, and a team of interested educators. Middle colleges are high schools fully housed on community college or university campuses. As a nationally organized consortium, they exist to encourage at-risk youth to succeed through three major supports: visible peer models, that is, students enrolled at the colleges; small classes; and superior academic and support services. These schools require completion of an internship program, modeled on LaGuardia College's core cooperative education program, leading students to success by connecting schooling with work opportunities.

Middle college high schools (MCHSs) are designed to help potential dropouts succeed at high school and go on to higher education or advanced training. They admit students who have been identified by their counselors and teachers as at-risk students with the potential for eventual college studies. From New York to California, middle college collaborations have resulted in similar positive student outcomes (National Middle College High School Consortium, 1999):

- Improved school attendance
- Improved grade point averages
- Significantly higher graduation rates

NEW DIRECTIONS FOR COMMUNITY COLLEGES, no. 111, Fall 2000 © Jossey-Bass, a Wiley company

- Lower annual dropout rates
- Higher numbers of graduates going on to higher education
- Increased job placement rates

Records of consortium member schools reflect the positive impact of the total program, thereby constituting a validation of the shared approach used in these small schools.

MCHSs have opened as new schools to serve large urban school districts in New York, Boston, Chicago, Dallas, Memphis, and Los Angeles and multi-district settings in the Flint, Michigan; Pittsburgh, Pennsylvania; and Nashville, Tennessee areas. Other middle colleges have evolved from existing alternative education programs hosted at higher education sites.

In this chapter, representatives from two sites, the original high school collaborative, Middle College at LaGuardia Community College, and the first multidistrict modification of the middle college concept, Mott Middle College (Michigan), share insights into how to establish and sustain a middle college high school.

Collaboratively Develop a Concept

The work of developing a concept begins with a series of planning seminars, with representatives of the college, the board of education, and outside authorities and consultants, to brainstorm and explore mission and educational concepts. Seminars should address the dual questions, "What do we want to do, and how can we best do it?" The final concept should represent all stakeholders, be well reasoned, and have the support of leading authorities.

A solid concept paper outlines the middle college's mission, underscores the joint contributions and commitments of both institutions, and, most important, details key conceptual, curricular, and learning frameworks of the new school. While the actual writing of a concept paper can be delegated to the project director, it should be reviewed and refined by important stakeholders from both institutions. The concept paper also needs to answer the key questions of a prospective parent: "What makes this school better than others, and what will my child's education here, from entrance to graduation, look like?"

Middle College at LaGuardia experience. Janet Lieberman, LaGuardia professor and conceptualizer of the school, convened a series of discussion groups held off-campus in her home with nationally known educators, as well as representatives of the board of education and LaGuardia Community College, ensuring a solidly based concept with built-in support. These meetings established and detailed her original concept design.

Mott Middle College experience. A group of educators representing Mott Community College, Flint Community College, Genesee Intermediate School District (GISD), and community leaders formed a task force to study best practices for dropout prevention and intervention across the United States. Based on a commitment to collaborate on the identification, development, and implementation of a program to lower dropout rates among high-potential, at-risk youth in Genesee County, LaGuardia's middle college model was selected to be replicated on a county-wide basis in Michigan. Chery Wagonlander, founding principal of Mott MCHS, facilitated the development of an implementation plan that included these components: solutions to twelve major issues regarding modifying the middle college concept to meet Genesee County needs and regulations; the school's proposed mission, goals, and learner objectives; curriculum plan; and administrative council structure. During December 1990, Mott Community College's board of trustees and GISD's board of education adopted a resolution to collaborate on implementing and sustaining a K–14 public high school designed to serve disengaged adolescents in and around Genesee County.

Select the Liaison and Project Director

The key college liaison must be someone respected by the college's administration and faculty. The liaison from the board of education must have access to and the trust of key decision makers.

Middle College at LaGuardia experience. Principals of New York's middle college high schools are supervisory employees of the board of education. By waiving certain hiring procedures, however, college personnel are fully involved in the selection processes, from screening applicants through granting tenure.

Mott Middle College experience. A high school principal-planner was identified to work with an experienced college dean to design and open a middle college by collaborating with 350 community volunteers. A K–12 administrator was selected to supervise the development of the project congruent with state and local policies, laws, and procedures.

Prepare a Planning Budget and Secure Funding

In addition to paying salaries and released time of liaisons, the budget should include adequate planning space, supplies, support services, and, most important, funds for faculty members from both institutions to serve as consultants during the planning process. A joint drawing account can be established for the project director that is not micromanaged by either institution.

Middle College at LaGuardia experience. In opening new schools, the Board of Education selects and hires project directors at least six months, and usually a full year, prior to the school's opening. Legislative money devoted to the schools is commonly advanced by the host college to allow the project director to hire college personnel as consultants and planners to work with the teaching staff.

Mott Middle College experience. The principal for Mott MCHS was identified a year before the school was expected to open. Flint Community Schools became the fiscal agent in order to receive full state aid for each student (regardless of their feeder school district) accepted into the program. The countywide GISD became the recipient of 90 percent of the total full-time-equivalent personnel needed to operate the project, taking on such responsibilities as staffing, arranging for teaching and learning materials, transportation, fees, technology, and equipment. Mott Community College provided the furnished facilities, nonconsumable materials and equipment, in-kind administration, and partial office, security, and student work-study costs.

Lay Foundations for School-Based Management and Internal Governance

The success of a school depends on ownership by all participants. Engendering wholehearted commitment, dedicated work, and a sense of ownership by all participants toward the school's outcomes and structures should predate the school's opening. Many schools vest heavy personnel powers, curricular decisions, and school-life decisions in permanent faculty and administration committees, ensuring continuity and institutionalization. College representation on these committees may also be helpful. Roles of the committees may change over the years, but they should start with clear missions and sets of responsibilities.

Middle College at LaGuardia experience. Since 1989, Middle College has formalized its governance structure into a school-based management team with teacher, parent, student, and administrative representation. The principal is the team chairperson, and decisions are made by consensus. The team meets weekly and issues minutes following each management meeting.

Mott Middle College experience. Since its planning stages, Mott MCHS has been the ongoing creation of a research-based learning community, governed by multiple educational institutions in cooperation with a school team consisting of representatives from the Flint schools, Mott Community College, the GISD, students, parents, and community members. Decisions are site based and founded in choice theory. The principal is the key liaison among all of these vested groups.

Profile and Recruit Faculty and Staff

Successful hiring occurs when the project director and planning staff profile the ideal staff members and then use these hiring criteria. Profiles vary depending on the mission of the school. Some schools need people capable of teaching more than one subject; others need single-subject-area specialists. Some schools require multigrade experience, experience in curriculum planning and writing, advisory or guidance experience, or demonstrated capabilities in interdisciplinary or activity-centered instruction.

Middle College at LaGuardia experience. All hiring at Middle College is done by a faculty committee that screens applicants, reviews applicants' portfolios, views demonstration lessons, interviews likely candidates, and makes final decisions about hiring.

Mott Middle College experience. Faculty, support staff, and administrators are hired by a committee process that includes representatives from current personnel, students, the school improvement team, and any others deemed important. Suitability to the middle college program is evaluated based on portfolio presentations, on-site curriculum writing products, videotapes of discussion time with Mott MCHS students, interviews, and reference checks. Final candidates are recommended to GISD's superintendent, who has the final authority to approve or deny placement.

Design Instructional Programs: Outline Scope and Sequence of the Curriculum

The scope of the curriculum refers to the curricular units or blocks of the school. Will they be single subject or interdisciplinary? Comprise traditional courses or new designs, such as internships? Mirror the district's traditional curriculum or seek new means to exceed old goals and objectives? What preparation do students need for internships? Which courses demand sequential learning? The sequence refers to the order in which learning takes place. Using the project's reputation as a new, innovative program, planners can experiment with new designs and new curricular parameters. With solidly based support, a middle college high school can achieve designs beyond the means of older schools.

Middle College at LaGuardia experience. Now widely replicated, Middle College's internship program was unique for nearly two decades, as were its cooperative education program and many of its interdisciplinary courses. Because a change process was also institutionalized at Middle College, the school is now expanding new modes of activity-centered instruction and alternative assessment.

Mott Middle College experience. Every Mott MCHS course has been created by the school's administration and teachers or is a result of national curriculum projects with other consortium MCHSs. Students are placed by skill level, mastery of content knowledge, and credit distribution needs. Instruction is highly facilitative; courses are usually team taught and interdisciplinary in nature, and assessment stresses the authentic application of newly acquired knowledge, skills, and processes. Dual enrollment in college courses is common and purposely placed into the curricular sequencing of each student's educational plan.

Design a Holistic, Integrated Pupil Personnel System

A progressive alternative high school demonstrates that "pupil personnel" means more than adding a cadre of counselors. It requires a holistic system for supporting and educating students. In addition, differing students' needs can be accommodated in various ways. An educated adult can provide much informal guidance, while formal counseling must be left to trained professionals. Most important, systems must ensure that students are always in close contact with adults who keep track of their successes and failures.

Middle College at LaGuardia experience. Each student at LaGuardia Middle College belongs to a homeroom, which meets regularly with a teacher. All ten homerooms are served by a comprehensive guidance team (a social worker and neighborhood worker) who meet with homeroom teachers to discuss individual students and design follow-up outreach or group counseling for students needing assistance. Every faculty member of the school, including the principal, can serve as a homeroom teacher.

Mott Middle College experience. Every teacher at Mott MCHS is hired and trained to be an adviser to students first and a teacher of content second. The student body is divided into focus groups led by teachers, which consume six and a half hours per week of instructional time designed to meet the affective needs of the students. Trained guidance counselors, student advocates, and career-to-work specialists provide individual and small group interventions and long-term counseling. Choice theory and reality therapy provide the philosophical base from which decisions and methods are chosen to deal with emotional, social, and cognitive issues.

Plan Ongoing, Systemic Outreach to Parents

Parents whose children have been unsuccessful in school need information about when the students are doing well and when they are doing poorly. Ideally, parents should be included in routine, quarterly progress meetings with teachers and counselors. Both "paper" and "people" systems must ensure that students are monitored and that problems are quickly detected and communicated.

Middle College at LaGuardia experience. Among Middle College's most successful programs is a parents' support group, with meetings hosted by the high school's social workers and counselors to allow parents to share problems and successes with their children. Parents were more likely to participate in these sessions than in old-fashioned parent-teacher associations. In June an orientation session is held for incoming students and their parents. This is followed by an August "patio" program for new students, with parents invited to attend lunch on the third and final day. The presence of a school neighborhood worker on each pupil personnel team ensures a constant flow of information to parents, including home visits, when necessary.

Mott Middle College experience. Parent communication is enhanced by Mott MCHS's attendance reports every two weeks, academic reports every four weeks, semester teacher conference days, and end-of-the-year annual reenrollment meetings. Individual teacher offices and telephones encourage frequent discourse between instructors and parents. School publications are designed to focus on the needs of parents. An organization has coalesced including active membership among parents, grandparents, teachers, students, and Mott administrators. Parents are pulled into the Mott team by frequent communication initiated by all Mott staff members. In addition, parents (as well as other family members) serve on curriculum development groups, make presentations in classes, and participate actively in all extracurricular activities. The power of serving the whole family has paid off in reengaging our youth.

Seek Long-Term Collaborative Funding or Establish a Collaborative Fund

Collaboration works best when it is supported by long-term, discretionary funding used solely to promote joint ventures: paying for joint college–high school staff development, paying college personnel as adjuncts in high school classes, paying tuition fees for high schoolers to take college courses if the college cannot donate or waive such fees, and providing joint conferences and governance meetings. Ongoing per-pupil funding, based on the school district's average per-pupil costs, ensures the establishment of the school and prevents outsiders or other decision makers from looking at the project as an expensive add-on in lean budget years.

Middle College at LaGuardia experience. The New York State legislature provides annual support grants to New York's middle colleges. Each year, the host college works with the principal to determine monies to be set aside for joint curriculum projects, supporting adjuncts teaching in the high school, and other cooperatively developed and operated programs. This funding also defrays some of the college's overhead and realty costs.

Mott Middle College experience. By working as a collaborative partner in the National Middle College High School Consortium, Mott MCHS has benefited as a recipient of grant funds to support curriculum development projects that use college adjuncts as team teachers with K–12 instructors. In addition, successful state and private foundation grant proposals have supported the development of multiple pilot programs that have become self-sustaining.

Locate and Acquire Suitable Space

A collaborative high school benefits when the space is shared by students of both institutions. However, the new school must have its own core space or hub: that is, its own administrative office, teachers' offices, student lounge, and meeting rooms. College and high school classrooms can be interspersed and flexibly used depending on the scheduling demands of both institutions. Integrating high school and college classrooms deepens the maturity and growth of high school-aged youngsters and college students' sense of mentoring and ownership.

Middle College at LaGuardia experience. Middle College's classrooms are interspersed with college classrooms arrayed around a central, support core of rooms in a college building. Because 30 percent of the school's students are off campus in internships, space needs are minimized, and, since both high school and college students use college specialty rooms (gyms, laboratories, cafeterias), space utilization is increased.

Mott Middle College experience. Similar to other middle colleges, Mott MCHS has a dedicated office hub and three classrooms that house an art classroom, school-to-work college center, and steel drum band program. Each semester, high school classes and events are scheduled after college classes and programs, allowing for daily interaction among adult learners. The high school budget reimburses the college for consumable supplies, damaged materials, and college work-study student time.

Find Ways to Mix and Match Personnel

Collaboration can be furthered if college personnel teach part time in the high school, offering electives or special courses; if high school teachers can be adjunct college faculty; if the principal of the school can hold administrative status, perhaps as a department chair, in the college; and if ongoing responsibilities such as curriculum development and staff development can be jointly planned and implemented.

Middle College at LaGuardia experience. The principal annually receives funds to hire college personnel, part time, for special curriculum projects or to teach courses, greatly expanding the range of courses available to the high school students. In addition, qualified high school teachers may receive adjunct appointments within the college.

Mott Middle College experience. The principal serves on the college president's cabinet and reports on a regular basis to the college vice president for academics. Grant funds and released time have allowed college instructors to form teams in the high school and high school teachers to team with college faculty. High school faculty with master's degrees in their content area are encouraged to seek adjunct instructor status with the host college and four-year universities that are hosted by Mott Community College.

Profile, Locate, and Recruit the Right Students

A school hosted on a college campus can easily become an elitist haven for a school district's better students, and if the students are not properly selected, a town-and-gown gulf can appear on the campus. The goal is to select students whose socioeconomic and academic histories parallel those of the host college's students, enhancing the chances that the college can properly serve the students and allowing for maximum mentoring possibilities.

Middle College at LaGuardia experience. All five of New York City's original middle college high schools were designed for high-risk students unlikely to graduate from high school. LaGuardia Community College serves many students unable to gain immediate admission into four-year colleges and many adult learners who have discontinued learning in the past. The typical middle college entrant has failed three or more foundational courses in math or English, and been truant more than forty days during the last year of junior high or middle school. Most are from working-class families, as are LaGuardia's students.

Mott Middle College experience. All students admitted to Mott MCHS have either dropped out of school or are perceived by themselves, parents, educators, or other professionals as highly at risk of doing so. Students represent all socioeconomic levels, geographic locales, and ethnicities found in Genesee County. Student applicants are tested for academic potential and the social maturity to handle the openness of an inner-city college campus.

Develop and Define an Understandable Admissions Process

Recruiting works best when done by a systematic routine, not open application, each year. In addition, indicators such as counselors' informal assessments of youngsters may be more reliable than traditional assessments such as grade point averages. Building strong relationships with administrators, faculty, and counselors in a few feeder schools can ensure a steady source of students who are likely to benefit from the programs. The college, high school staff, and feeder schools and districts should all jointly develop a profile of students for whom the middle college is intended and a process by which such students will be recruited and admitted.

Middle College at LaGuardia experience. Approximately 80 percent of Middle College's students are identified by guidance counselors and recommended by administrators from fewer than a dozen middle or junior high schools. The high school maintains collaboration with these schools by holding annual preadmissions open houses for middle school personnel and holding all student-parent open houses in the middle schools, ensuring that middle school personnel maintain ownership of selecting students. Interested applicants are also invited to "student for a day" programs at the high school, partly devoted to peer interviews by current middle college students. In practice, peer interviewers recommend admission of almost all applicants, but the process ensures buy-in by both the new students and current students.

Mott Middle College experience. All twenty-one school districts in Genesee County view Mott MCHS as an option for students who are identified as high potential and high risk. In order to maintain a small school that is also reflective of countywide demographics, the number of admissions slots recommended for each sending school is based on its population percentage in Genesee County. If openings are not used by one district, other non-county schools may make referrals. Students go through a collaborative admissions process that involves the feeder school, student, parents, and Mott officials. The student, a parent or guardian, and Mott must agree that the middle college is a meaningful option for a successful turnaround experience.

Potential students and parents are invited to information nights to review the formal admissions process, which includes academic testing, a student visit to campus, a parent interview, a student interview, and consultation with the feeder district's counselor or administrator. Depending on past history and assessed readiness to handle the open college environment, students are admitted with no limitations or placed in support groups or a modified probation plan.

Build a Communications Network of Key Constituents

A successful school shapes its future and its image by deciding who needs information about the school and when they need it, particularly those who are in a position to affect the future of a school: unions, legislators, administrators with decision-making power over the school, parents who do or will send their children to the school, community members, and the broader educational community.

Middle College at LaGuardia experience. Middle College keeps mailing lists of constituents who appreciate information about the school and whose decisions affect the school's future, from parents to legislators and political leaders. Some groups receive regular newsletters, while other individuals and groups receive one-time mailings in response to requests made of the school. Each constituency has different information needs, and Middle College has aimed to meet each group's needs.

Mott Middle College experience. Regular presentations are scheduled with the major community members who have the power and responsibility to affect policy and funding for Mott MCHS. In addition, key stakeholders (current students and their parents, graduates, former parents, area counselors and administrators, and county mental health and criminal justice professionals) are targeted for frequent communication. Information distribution about Mott MCHS is tailored to meet separate audience needs. Both public relations offices from the college and intermediate school district work in concert to keep the Mott MCHS concept, activities, and accomplishments in the limelight. An emphasis is placed on all school members taking the responsibility to share experiences and findings in continuing to build this school.

Conclusion

Experience has shown that establishing and sustaining middle college high schools depend on successful collaboration, shared governance, communication, administrative support, and energetic and visionary leadership. Every site, whether opened as a new school or the result of a rollover from an existing program, develops and maintains itself first and foremost by modeling best practices of educators who view themselves as teachers and leaders, willing to do the personal and professional work necessary to bring about positive results. An institutional commitment to divert and protect sufficient funds for ongoing staff development focused on cross-site collaboration protects the potential for maintaining excellence in teaching and learning as well as serving as models for future high school–college collaborations.

Reference

National Middle College High School Consortium. *Member Schools: Annual Outcomes Data Report.* Long Island City, N.Y.: National Middle College High School Consortium, 1999.

CECILIA L. CUNNINGHAM *is principal of Middle College High School at LaGuardia Community College and the director of the National Middle College High School Consortium.*

CHERY S. WAGONLANDER *is principal of the Mott Middle College at Mott Community College.*

6

Student support services at high schools and community colleges can work together to design programs to assist students in their transition to higher education.

Working with Schools to Ease Student Transition to the Community College

Lemuel Watson

Educators in high schools and community colleges face the challenge of creating optimal learning environments for students. Creating these environments for high school students requires that student support personnel, faculty members, and administrators acquire as much knowledge as possible about students' personal background, community environment, and motivation in order to assist them as they make the transition to college (Watson, 1996; Watson and Stage, 1999). This chapter offers practical advice on how schools and colleges can work collaboratively to ease this transition, focusing particularly on the role of student support services in the transitional period.

The term *student support* encompasses the work of those professionals, including some faculty members, who are responsible for serving students beyond the in-class experience. Because these professionals are concerned with developing the students in a holistic manner, they must involve themselves in the total education of students: teaching students how to be better learners and how to think critically in order to solve the problems they encounter both in and out of the classroom. They must also assist faculty members and other institutional agents in their quest to teach new students how to take responsibility for their actions.

Building Transitional Partnerships

Programs that assist in the transition from high school to community college need to target students beginning in early elementary school. In fact, building partnerships to include the whole community is often a wise move for community colleges because these initiatives make the college both a provider of learning and a force for economic development. In addition, collaborations with industry provide funding and support for precollege programs and apprenticeships (Becherer and Becherer, 1998).

Collaborations between student support units, families, communities, and secondary schools have recently begun to attract the attention of those who construct learning environments for college students (Lempert, 1995). For example, the Institute for Development of Educational Activities recently sponsored a conference that afforded educators an opportunity to discuss existing partnerships between public schools, university faculty members, the business community, and students in colleges of education. Many of the seminars focused on the nature of interinstitutional collaboration. Topics discussed included cultural differences between higher education and K-12 schools, policy issues, and collaboration as a structure for learning (Harper and Harston, 1996). By expanding our traditional boundaries to include secondary schools, businesses, and the larger community, student services professionals can begin to better understand students and their transitional needs before they arrive on the college campus (Terrell and Watson, 1996; Weidman, 1989).

O'Banion and Gillett-Karam (1996) encourage community colleges to seize opportunities for extended involvement with the cities, towns, and villages in which they are located. Such deep involvement is evident in one community college's Project Start Trek, held for area eighth graders. Using creative, entertaining, and age-appropriate programs, the college introduces nearly six thousand eighth graders to various professional and career opportunities, encourages them to pursue higher education, and reinforces the value of basic skills (math, reading, and writing). More important, this program encourages students to think about their lifelong goals and desired lifestyle and to make the connection between lifestyle and the education needed to achieve a desired living standard.

Types of Transition Assistance

When creating new collaborative programs, student services professionals must try to minimize duplication of resources. Determining whether K-12 organizations, community agencies, or other institutions of higher education have similar programs may be of help before instituting a new program. During professional development activities, the community college needs to extend invitations to local high schools and universities to become part of the learning community. This joint work can take many forms.

Addressing Academic Readiness. One example of student support efforts undertaken on an interinstitutional basis to assist in the transition process is found in the collaborative work of the Seminole County Public Schools and Seminole Community College (SCC), located in Sanford, Florida. To help prepare middle and high school students for college, SCC's student services office established several unique partnerships that focus on career and academic readiness (Culp, 1998). The college's 2+2+2 program draws on educators from K–12 and postsecondary institutions to create a seamless transitional process for prospective students. Student services professionals begin to work with sophomores in local high schools by giving them a placement test that profiles their academic skills and alerts them to deficiencies that may hinder their academic progress. The intent is to minimize the need for remediation once students get to the college.

New Student Orientation. Orientation, one of the most important services for students at any college, provides students an opportunity to ask questions and solve problems before they begin their studies. It also helps students make connections with other people and units within the college. An orientation program that includes faculty, counselors, and administrators from the community college and surrounding high schools is especially helpful, allowing both groups to educate the students and each other about the expectations of college life. This interinstitutional approach differs from standard orientation practices in which the college alone provides assessment, advising, and registration.

Cook (1996) compiled a list of model programs for orientation at community colleges to show the variety and creativity that some student services personnel are demonstrating. Most do not take the interinstitutional approach, but they embrace a comprehensive approach to orientation that could easily involve representatives from local schools—for example:

Johnson County Community College (Kansas) has an eight-week orientation program that operates daily during the summer and includes help with admissions, assessment, and registration. Students get everything they need in one place to begin their work at the college.

Miami Dade Community College invites all new students for orientation during the spring and summer, and all new students are required to take the first-year-experiences course.

Orientation at William Rainey Harper College (Illinois) consists of three parts: preenrollment assessment, guidelines, policies, and procedure information, and an introduction to multiculturalism; registration, which is led by paraprofesssionals who guide the new students through the process and match at-risk students with a mentor; and a program titled "The Freshman Experience," which is held the Sunday prior to the start of classes and includes, among other activities, a motivational speaker and information about campus life.

Muskegon Community College (Michigan) student service professionals begin orientation in the high school with a skills assessment test and an abbreviated introduction to the college.

Orientation is one of the most important processes in the transition from high school to college. Therefore, student services professionals and faculty members must be clear and concise about their expectations for student behavior in college. Students need to be informed that they must be active learners and take responsibility for their own lives and their academic success. This message must be conveyed along with the college's policies, rules, and regulations within a short period of time. Presentations led by student services professionals to large groups may not be the most effective means of structuring orientation. Instead, counselors can work with students in small groups to provide the individual attention that most students need.

Counselor-to-Counselor Activities. The counselor, academic adviser, or adviser is one of the most important persons whom students encounter in the transition from high school to community college. The adviser in community colleges helps students clarify personal and educational goals, directs them to the resources that will be beneficial for their success, and provides support for academic and personal problems. Pineda and Bowes (1995) recognize that the adviser role is crucial to the overall objectives of the community college. The advising center is the only structured service on campus that guarantees students interact with a concerned representative.

Some college counseling staffs conduct regularly scheduled meetings with their high school counterparts to exchange information, share resources, and generally develop professional rapport among themselves. At Heartland Community College (Illinois), the student support staff meets with area high school counselors and superintendents each year to inform them of changes and to get feedback on a number of situations that could benefit students and the college. In addition, the college catalogue and personnel directory are distributed to high school counselors, giving them access to the appropriate college personnel who can address specific questions or problems.

Another initiative at Seminole Community College is the effort to work with counselors at middle and elementary schools to establish a career counseling program for students (Culp, 1998). This program is designed to encourage students to think about their job prospects early and to show them how career decisions determine the course work and skills they need to enter a profession. This program also allows students access to the resources that will help them understand various career options and how they might best determine their career goals. SCC's student services professionals and faculty members provide workshops and manuals to public school counselors.

Addressing Out-of-Class Concerns. To support the transition from school to college, student support personnel at both the K-12 and postsecondary levels can help students recognize that their learning in the classroom is related to their out-of-class lives. Dialogue with students about what and how they are learning (Whitt, 1994), as well as programs that help students draw connections between their real-world lives and what they have learned in class (Schroeder and Hurst, 1996), are avenues for increasing the chances of a successful transition. Therefore, faculty and student services professionals need to be well equipped to deal with the diverse student backgrounds found at community colleges.

Professional Development. Providing additional professional development training and support ensures the availability of qualified professionals who can intelligently discuss the transition process with students and diagnose their specific problems. Many community colleges have teaching and learning centers, technology and learning centers, or staff development centers for this purpose. Staff development can also take place in cooperation with the schools. In central Illinois, for example, high schools, community colleges, and universities are linked to an interactive television network that provides training, course work, and videoconferencing for the entire educational community. Such systems can strengthen collaborative efforts between high schools and community colleges. For example, they can be used to facilitate detailed training sessions, conducted by student services personnel, that will help high school counselors understand college expectations for entering students. This type of effort requires a considerable fiscal commitment in terms of both dollar allocation and staff release time.

Conclusion

Honors, bridge-type, career, and early-start programs are ways in which community colleges help high school students make the transition to higher education. These efforts are strengthened to the extent that they evolve collaboratively with feeder schools, as well as with other community organizations. As Chen, Konantz, Rosenfeld, and Frost discuss in Chapter Eight, community partnerships also provide support for underprepared and at-risk students, helping the public schools prepare these students for postsecondary academic coursework. Yet the literature provides only a starting point; it does not address the unique circumstances of location or personality. Each community college and its surrounding schools form a unique educational network; none is quite like another. Within these networks, individual students bring their unique characteristics. The transition to college seems to begin at different times for different students, and the adjustment to college also depends on the student's own development.

Interinstitutional collaboration can help educators in local communities identify the unique challenges they face and determine the most effective ways of meeting those challenges. For example, how information is filtered from the community college to the high school counselor, the teacher, and, finally, the student plays a major part in the transition process. But the procedure for disseminating needed information in an urban environment may be quite different from that used in a rural environment. Different approaches may also be needed when dealing with honors students on the one hand and students with academic deficiencies on the other. Determining these approaches, as well as other strategies in facilitating students' transition to postsecondary education, is a shared obligation of the college and its neighboring schools.

References

Becherer, J. J., and Becherer, J. H. "Nest for Dreams, Backdrops for Visions: Making a Difference with Students." In M. M. Culp and St. R. Helfgot (eds.), *Life at the Edge of the Wave.* Washington, D.C.: National Association of Student Personnel Administrators, 1998.

Butte Community College Secondary/Postsecondary Articulation: The Partnership Concept, the Partnership in Action, and Highlights of the Partnership in Action. Oroville, Calif.: Butte College, 1990.

Cook, L. P. "Building a Path: Orientation as the Critical Link to Student Success." In J. N. Hankin (ed.), *The Community College: Opportunity and Access for America's First-Year Students.* Columbia, S.C.: National Resource Center for the Freshman Year Experience and Students in Transition, University of South Carolina, 1996.

Culp, M. M. "Infiltrating Academe." In M. M. Culp and St. R. Helfgot (eds.), *Life at the Edge of the Wave.* Washington, D.C.: National Association of Student Personnel Administrators, 1998.

Harper, J., and Harston, A. "K-16 Collaboration: University Professionals of Illinois and the Chicago Teacher Union." *University,* 1996, *21,* 4–7.

Lempert, D. H. *Escape from the Ivory Tower. Student Adventures in Democratic Experiential Education.* San Francisco: Jossey-Bass, 1995.

O'Banion, T., and Gillett-Karam, R. "The People's College and the Street People: Community Colleges and Community Development." *Community College Journal,* 1996, *68,* 11–15.

Pineda, E. N., and Bowes, G. "Multicultural Campuses: The Challenge for Community College Counselors." *Community College Journal of Research and Practice,* 1995, *19,* 151–160.

Schroeder, C. C., and Hurst, J. C. "Designing Learning Environments That Integrate Curricular and Cocurricular Experiences." *Journal of College Student Development,* 1996, *37*(2), 174–81.

Terrell, M., and Watson, L. "Collaborative Partnerships for a Diverse Campus Community." *Journal of College Student Development,* 1996, *37,* 249–253.

Watson, L. W. "A Collaborative Approach to Student Learning." *Planning and Changing: An Educational Leadership and Policy Journal,* 1996, *27,* 165–179.

Watson, L. W., and Stage, F. K. "A Framework to Enhance Student Learning." In Frances K. Stage, Lemuel W. Watson, and Melvin Terrell (eds.), *Enhancing Student Learning: Setting the Campus Context.* Washington, D.C.: National Association of Student Personnel Administrators, 1999.

Weidman, J. "Undergraduate Socialization: A Conceptual Approach." In J. Smart (ed.), *Higher Education: Handbook of Theory and Research.* New York: Agathon, 1989.

Whitt, E. J. "Encouraging Adult Learner Involvement." *NASPA Journal,* 1994, *31,* 309–318.

LEMUEL W. WATSON is associate professor of higher education at Clemson University.

7

*After assessment tests identify the inadequate preparation
of local high school graduates for college, a partnership
forms between the local community college and school
district to address the needs of at-risk students.*

Working with Schools to Prepare Students for College: A Case Study

*Charlene R. Nunley, Mary Kay Shartle-Galotto,
Mary Helen Smith*

> Educators must take the lead in establishing the environment for
> learning.
>
> K. Patricia Cross (1998)

The past decade has brought a tremendous increase in partnerships between school systems and colleges. Although these two groups historically have acknowledged their interdependence, for the most part the two entities remained isolated. In recent years, several factors, including changes in employer expectations, a move to mass education, and a concern for the inadequate preparation of high school graduates, have rendered previous partnership efforts inappropriate for meeting the educational urgencies of today. There is a dawning realization among college administrators that some of the responsibility for inadequate preparation of high school students lies with them.

The issue of underprepared students arriving in higher education has moved to center stage because of media interest in these students and attempts by politicians to scale back public dollars for remedial course work in public two- and four-year colleges. Nationally, about 40 percent of students enrolling in community colleges require remediation in math, reading, or writing (Smith and others, 1997).

Offering developmental classes for underprepared students is not a new phenomenon. Colleges have routinely offered writing and math classes to balance differences in preparation among incoming freshmen; even among the Ivy League colleges, developmental offerings were historically an accepted practice (Larson, Garies, and Campbell, 1996).

However, since 1945, the advent of open admissions in some public colleges and the newly formed community colleges has made the issue of academic preparation more critical. The gap between high school graduation and college readiness became more visible and has continued to widen. Some students who had completed the required units of English and math in high school found that their skills were not sufficient to succeed in college-level writing and math. Even more troubling were mounting data demonstrating that many of these high school graduates had moderate to severe reading deficiencies.

State Attention

Active K–16 initiatives to analyze the transition between high school and college have developed in a number of states, including California, Georgia, Maryland, Nebraska, Oregon, and Texas. The Maryland Partnership for Teaching and Learning—K–16 provides an admirable example. Education Secretary Nancy Grasmick, Higher Education Secretary Patricia Florestano, and University System of Maryland Chancellor Donald Langenberg created this partnership. Its objectives include raising standards throughout K–16 education and ensuring that public school and college programs are well articulated, thereby increasing the number of high school graduates who are fully prepared for college-level work. It has reviewed and made significant recommendations regarding the following issues:

- The future of teacher education
- Appropriate skill levels for the new high school assessment programs (a series of tests that will determine high school graduation by the middle of this decade)
- Sequencing of high school and college curricula in math and English
- Improving the college readiness of high school graduates

Statewide research projects were initiated by the Remedial Education Subcommittee of the Maryland K–16 Council. The subcommittee interviewed focus groups of students enrolled in remedial classes in several institutions across the state, asking for their perspectives on why they were in remedial classes. The researchers were surprised to find that the students did not blame their schools, their teachers, their family circumstances, or the placement test for the fact that they needed remediation. They took responsibility for themselves. They told the researchers the following things:

- They did not take high school seriously.
- They purposely did not take challenging classes.
- Their major reason for going to school was to socialize.

- They were not motivated in high school.
- They did not think that college was in their future.
- They took an "I don't care" attitude beginning in about tenth grade.
- They would like to help other students avoid their mistakes.

This information made it clear there was a need to undertake joint school-college activities designed to get students' attention back on the fact that their high school educational experience had real consequences for their future. It was also apparent that information needed to be communicated to students and parents about the pathways of courses that do lead to college readiness and those that do not. This state research and Montgomery County's local research shaped the array of initiatives that followed.

Legislative Attention

In 1999, for the first time, the issue of local schools and postsecondary partnerships caught the attention of Maryland's state legislature. Several legislators attended a conference where they learned that Maryland was a leader in K–16. Several powerful legislators have developed a bill that would provide significant financial support for K–16 initiatives. Because the price tag of the legislation is high, the bill was not passed this session but is being reviewed and refined during the summer legislative recess, with a major initiative then emerging in the next legislative session. If this bill does eventually pass, it will overcome one of the major policy barriers to progress in school-college partnerships: a lack of financial resources allocated for this goal.

Maryland continues to move forward on a number of fronts to assess, analyze, and improve the state's educational structure. In 1990, the Maryland Higher Education Commission (MHEC) approved the statewide compilation of data related to the progress of Maryland high school graduates through the first year of college at state universities and colleges. The resultant *Student Outcome and Achievement Report* (SOAR), which was released in 1994, was intended to provide feedback to public high school principals, parents, and local decision makers regarding objective measures of school performance.

Despite steadily accumulating research and predictions by educational analysts regarding changing demographics, an altered workplace, and increasing pressure to pursue education after high school, Montgomery County received its first SOAR information with stunned disbelief. Montgomery County, with a reputation for affluence, a nationally recognized public school system, and more than double the national percentage of adults with post–high school degrees, was not prepared to hear that 57 percent of Montgomery County Public School (MCPS) graduates enrolling in Montgomery College required math remediation and almost 40 percent were not reading at college level. The class of 1993, as documented in the 1994 SOAR data, was the first to be assessed on college entrance by ACCUPLACER, an Educational Testing Service standardized test selected as the placement instrument at the college.

MCPS, at that time serving 125,000 students in 21 high schools, 26 middle schools, and 123 elementary schools, had gradually moved from a 94 percent white student body in 1968 to a campus population that was now 19 percent African American, 12 percent Asian, 12 percent Hispanic, and 57 percent white. Free or reduced-price meal service was provided for 29 percent of the students, and in every school English for Speakers of Other Languages (ESOL) services were being provided to almost eight thousand students.

Montgomery College, with three geographically separate campuses, was enrolling about twenty-two thousand credit students. Approximately one in four MCPS graduates enrolls at the college within a year of graduation. Montgomery College has historically maintained an open admissions policy and, like 91 percent of two-year colleges, offers extensive developmental services to students not academically prepared for college-level work. Montgomery College instituted the use of ACCUPLACER in 1993 in response to a state mandate to begin systematic assessment and placement of students using one of three state-approved standardized instruments.

Partnership Initiation

Although Montgomery College and MCPS were under the direction of the Montgomery County Board of Education until 1965, the two institutions were pursuing somewhat sequential but separate missions by the early 1990s. Relationships, although cordial, did not regularly include close communication with regard to curriculum, professional development, or shared student data. Both institutions, however, had recently developed student success models, which were to form the foundation and shared vision of the future partnership.

Into this environment in the spring of 1994 the SOAR data arrived, generating intense interest and the inevitable questions by the local media. The *Washington Post, Montgomery Gazette,* and *Montgomery Journal* raised the obvious question. How could a highly acclaimed school system with a $900 million budget graduate large numbers of students assessed as underprepared by the local community college? Anxiety was widespread, as MCPS sought to explain how students could have been identified in such large numbers by ACCUPLACER. Montgomery College faculty and administration reviewed the test data with some trepidation, and parents and local decision makers demanded answers.

Response by the Institutions

Both the college and the school system were somewhat restrained in publicly assigning blame, and discussions began on how to enlist the energy of the county's entire education community to work toward greater academic success for all students. County Council members urged the superintendent of schools and the president of the college to review collaborative efforts, and in response, the superintendent and the president began a series of lunch meetings. Upon realizing that the college served a quarter of the school system's graduating classes, the two called for school and college staff to begin a joint review of data, with the purpose of identifying strategies for closing the newly prominent achievement gap between high school graduation and college requirements. Support continued to grow as the board of education and the college trustees also began meeting together and agreed that the two systems could serve students best by joining their expertise and resources.

A research study conducted in 1995 identified common strategies that could be jointly implemented to improve student preparation and performance. The college and the school representatives decided to integrate databases from both institutions to compare the high school course sequences and academic achievement levels of students who tested as needing remediation at the community college with those who did not. The research was extraordinarily useful and unequivocal in determining that three pathways through high school exist in Montgomery County.

Pathway One leads to college readiness for virtually all students who follow it. These students complete mathematics through at least the precalculus level and participate in honors English classes. Pathway Two leads to remediation for one in three students. These students take intermediate algebra or trigonometry as their highest-level mathematics courses and nonhonors twelfth-grade English. Pathway Three leads to remediation for virtually every student who follows it. These students complete high school mathematics only through geometry and as seniors often take an English course that is below grade level. These data prepared the way for changes necessary to increase the college readiness of high school graduates.

As a result of this major finding, students who prepare seriously for college and take rigorous courses have a very low risk of being placed into remedial or developmental classes upon entering college. A series of recommendations were developed that formed the framework for a new partnership. Among the recommendations were these:

- Immediately focus on student readiness at the high school level.
- Provide direct, supportive counseling services at the time of college registration.
- Conduct an ongoing review of college placement criteria.
- Conduct follow-up research on post–high school performance.

Senior staff from both MCPS and Montgomery College moved rapidly to bring a collaborative plan to life. Encouraged by support from board members and local leaders, a bold plan emerged to bring the school system and the college together in a partnership to identify students who were not on track for college readiness and convey to students and parents the urgent need to address this matter. The plan included collaborative intervention strategies to change aspirations and enlist parents in a joint effort to prepare students for college-level work. Not only were students put on alert early in their high school careers, they were encouraged to consider and aspire to college enrollment.

In October 1996, a press conference, well attended because of ongoing interest in the SOAR data, was jointly called to announce the Partnership Initiative. The chief academic officer of the college pledged to bring early college assessment to partner high schools to let students know how they were progressing on skill acquisition. The deputy superintendent of MCPS vowed to support and fund a program of intervention and instruction to help identified students aspire high, work harder, and finish high school with stronger academic skills. Both institutions would support collaborative testing, research and follow-up, professional development, and curriculum sharing. Students, faculty, teachers, and staff would be encouraged to meld their perspectives and expertise to make a dramatic attempt to effect change quickly. The goal was ultimately to increase the college readiness of MCPS graduates. One area of collaboration identified for immediate attention was an early assessment project.

Early Assessment Testing

Three pilot high schools were chosen to begin the early-warning testing. The entire tenth-grade cohort of students would be assessed using the Placement Articulation Software System (PASS), which provided ACCUPLACER high school norming information. This assessment would categorize sophomores as being on track for college readiness in two years, already meeting college-level expectations, or lagging behind for college readiness in some skill areas. This final category constituted those needing a wake-up call, and it was hoped that students so identified would be responsive to efforts to get them into rigorous course work and supportive advising and counseling. The testing, which involved about fifteen hundred tenth graders, was administered on site at Montgomery College campuses and in some of the pilot high schools.

Further Collaborative Efforts

Although the tenth-grade testing was the most high-profile and labor-intensive aspect of the new partnership, other collaborative efforts were launched almost immediately:

Research. Four projects were outlined to follow the progress of students assessed in the pilot.

Curriculum. High school teachers and college faculty began meeting regularly to review curriculum objectives and standards of progress in English, mathematics, and reading.

Intervention. An intervention package was developed that included a jointly taught after-school course, "Future Focus," for students identified in the "alert" category of PASS testing reporting. A high school English teacher and a college counselor developed and team-taught this class in the high schools. Several sections were offered to students who had been identified as lagging behind. The goal was not to remediate but to focus student aspirations on college readiness.

Funding. Staff from the college and MCPS collaborated on developing and applying to external funding sources for resources to support the partnership plans.

Implementation Hurdles

By the late spring of 1997, the partnership was flourishing, and counterparts at every level—supervisors and deans, counselors and guidance staff, teachers and faculty, and students from high school and college—were all communicating, sharing, and deepening their understanding of colleagues and fellow students.

The implementation stage had been fitful, at times awkward, and sometimes even hilarious as the two cumbersome bureaucracies attempted to adapt gracefully to midcourse corrections. Getting the information out to the entire tenth grade, their teachers, parents, counselors, and bus drivers, as well as to the assessment personnel, faculty, and staff in three large high schools was an exhausting and only moderately successful effort the first time it was done. Students, not understanding this "new" test, did not take it seriously in one school. Another school had to be switched at the last moment because the principal chose not to continue. Finally, endless meetings ensued to determine how, when, and in what format to notify parents of results. Schools found themselves in the sensitive position of telling parents of students who regularly received A's that their children's reading or writing skills (or both) would not achieve college readiness at the present rate of progress. Despite the many crises and daily challenges, both Montgomery College and MCPS staff were beginning to appreciate and value the collaboration and to view the effort as a great boon and incentive for students.

Another challenge was raised by the media. A series of articles mounted by a local reporter demanded to know how schools participating in the pilot compared with each other. Principals and assessment staff protested that the purpose of the PASS assessment was to provide a personal and individual assessment profile to the student for advising purposes. Comparing the performances of participating schools would be meaningless. Nevertheless, newspaper articles continued to deplore the "secret test scores" and to demand aggregate, and hence comparative, data. Board members were closely questioned as to the content of the tests, and principals threatened to withdraw from the effort if the purpose of testing continued to be misconstrued. For a few tense weeks, staff feared the efforts would be dismantled to avoid inappropriate comparisons. Fortunately, the superintendent and board expressed confidence and support for the initiative while firmly refusing to compare school performance.

The first year of the partnership (1996-1997) ended on a high note as the final joint effort, the testing of twelfth-grade students from every county high school, was initiated. MCPS provided bus transportation to the college for any senior who wished to be assessed, advised, and registered at Montgomery College. The college set up testing, orientation, and advising sessions for visiting seniors and waived the application fee for participating students. No matter where students were planning to attend college, the placement information allowed them to plan and perhaps even to take a summer brush-up class if needed before beginning the fall semester. During the late spring, a completion ceremony was held on the Rockville campus for students who had participated in the tenth-grade intervention program. They came to campus with parents and teachers and received certificates, congratulations, and encouragement to continue to work hard and plan for college attendance. The academic year ended full of plans and optimism, and with a commitment to expand the tenth-grade testing gradually to all twenty-one high schools, offer more sections of "Future Focus," involve parents, mentor students, train peer tutors, and develop shared professional development courses. There was strong support for the collaboration from parents, teachers, and staff, and the potential benefits for students seemed endless. Plans were structured to support student achievement from several angles: instruction, counseling, parent involvement, financial, and peer contacts. Table 7.1 illustrates the interlocking collaborative plan for full implementation of partnership activities.

Beyond Remediation

In addition to focusing on preparing and advising potentially marginal students, the partnership opened up new avenues of opportunity and challenge for the students identified as college ready by the tenth-grade PASS testing. Several programs targeted students taking advanced placement classes who wanted to earn college credit as well as advanced placement. Still other high schools wanted to offer college courses on site to allow students to build a college transcript and earn credits while still in high school. All of these possibilities were implemented during the second year of this partnership (1997–1998). A new honors program was developed offering full scholarships and a summer-abroad experience to graduating seniors; 25 county students were selected from over 130 applicants.

Table 7.1. Montgomery College-Montgomery County Public Schools Partnership: A College Readiness Program

Target Students	Parents of Target Students	MCPS Counselors	MC Counselors	MCPS Teachers	MC Faculty
Assessed below grade level in reading. Need rigorous courses and additional support to be ready for college by high school graduation. Advised by MCPS counselors of scores. Urged to take rigorous courses in high school to improve college readiness. Recruited to "Future Focus." Recruited to mentoring project. Seniors recruited to take student development courses: "Career Development," "Study Skills," and "College Survival." Retested and advised in senior year.	Oriented to college success preparation program opportunities. Receive newsletter. Sign contract to support students in mentoring activities. Participate in college forums with students. Participate in financial aid seminars.	Recommend appropriate MCPS rigorous courses. Recommend college preparation program. Direct students to "Future Focus." Recommend students for mentoring program. Collaborate with MC counselors to reinforce college preparation.	Share scores with schools and counselors. Recruit and train MC student mentors. Monitor mentoring program. Participate in "Future Focus." Present college forum and student orientation.	Reinforce need to select challenging courses and work for improved reading skills. Encourage students to focus on college success preparation. Participate in developing and team-teaching "Future Focus." Take in-service course: "Teaching Reading and Writing in the Content Areas." Collaborate with MC faculty to disseminate successful strategies by means of a partnership Web site and presentations at the MC Critical Literacy Cherry Blossom Festival.	Develop and offer in-service course: "Teaching Reading and Writing in the Content Areas." Participate in developing, team-teaching, and evaluating "Future Focus." Collaborate with MCPS teachers to disseminate successful strategies by means of a partnership Web site and presentations at the MC Critical Literacy Cherry Blossom Conference.

Moving Ahead

In the fall of 1999, several factors galvanized the collaboration. A new president, the former chief academic officer, was appointed at the college, and a new superintendent was hired for the school system. The synergy between the new leaders was immediate, and the last barriers to progress began to disappear. Resources and personnel were moved into the partnership high schools to facilitate the intervention programs. Support and funds were made available to expand the testing and provide additional programs for identified and targeted students.

The partnership moved to a new level of significance in the fall of 1999 as the newly elected superintendent and the newly appointed president moved rapidly to prepare a joint budget to be presented to the County Council and the county executive to increase funding for the joint efforts at a much more extensive level. Staff from both institutions collaborated to identify the needs and possibilities that had been projected but were not fiscally possible during the prior three years. Outreach to parents, seminars for peer advising and tutoring, and greatly increased cooperation between teachers, counselors, and decision makers at all levels were built into the joint budget. Planning for joint curriculum review and development and a projected professional development institute were part of the intense discussion that went into the development of a joint budget document. Montgomery College has submitted a $1.2 million budget supplemental request, and MCPS has developed and submitted a similar request for funds. This budget has been supported and approved by the county executive and the County Council, and will fund a truly collaborative and integrated effort to narrow the gap between high school graduation and college readiness.

Factors Facilitating Collaboration Success

The most important factor that facilitated the formation of the initial partnership was a focus on student needs and student success at both the MCPS level and at Montgomery College. *Success for Every Student* was a policy document developed and approved within the school system to focus decisions and programs on facilitating outcomes that promoted individual success. At the college, a similar effort has produced the Student Success Model, which committed the resources and hooked each decision to the eventual impact on students and their success at the college.

In addition, both the school system and the college were faced with increasing diversity within the student body—diversity in race, income, ethnic background, native language, preparation level, and cultural attitudes toward education. It was clear to the leadership of both institutions that a joint effort to address these common problems would be more productive than ignoring or approaching these systemic issues alone. The two institutions have joined resources and grown in mutual respect as the dimensions of the problems and the gaps in preparation become more evident. The new superintendent issued an early report to the community, *Raising the Bar*, in which he pledged to bring resources and effort to every level of performance, with no excuses accepted and a common outcome for students from every background. The president of the college has pledged to work with the school system, build on the interest expressed by state legislators, and pursue funding for similar partnerships at the state level.

Factors Impeding This Collaboration

Despite commitment at the executive and the staff levels, obtaining support and commitment at the department, program, and instructional levels was a slow process. Many within the system resisted the new initiatives. Communication was difficult to achieve in two large and separate bureaucracies, and there was much resistance in moving the project through both institutions. In each organization, stereotypes and conventional wisdom died hard. A mystique had grown up around Montgomery College as a default or second-rate option for MCPS students, something suited only for the very poorest students. At the college, frequent conversations had characterized MCPS as both arrogant and incompetent in providing graduates with the requisite basic skills for college success.

Although partnerships of a similar nature can be found among some community colleges and school systems across the country, the possibilities have just begun to be recognized. A report from the Pew Bridge Project (Pew Charitable Trust, 1999) notes the need for these collaborative efforts:

> While educators and policy makers share the common goal of improving student performance, they often act in isolation; thus efforts are sometimes conflicting or duplicated, and often certain needs are never addressed. This is not the fault of a particular set of people or institutions. Rather, the current organization of secondary schools and universities is such that communication between levels is often difficult, if not impossible. Reform initiatives at different levels within the entire K-16 education system must be better integrated or the whole mission of increasing opportunities for all students for higher education could veer dangerously off course.

Some of the barriers that get in the way of any efforts include college faculty attitudes that students' preparation is a school system responsibility and colleges should not be involved. Some administrators and teachers in school systems do not respect their local community college and are not very open to accepting guidance from these institutions about the skill levels necessary for collegiate success. Pulling together two large bureaucracies to work jointly is a challenge; even identifying the right people from each organization to bring to the table is difficult. Allocating resources necessary to build partnership initiatives is often a barrier. Two organizations with different funding approaches and priorities need to commit to invest in this partnership or to convince political leaders to provide financial support. Most important, these partnerships will never be effective unless the senior leadership of both the college and the school system are deeply committed to a long-term effort to make the partnership work. Many barriers along the way will give participants an excuse for abandoning the partnership, but if the leadership stays involved and helps remove the barriers, the others will have no choice but to stay dedicated to improving collegiate preparation of students.

Conclusion

Looking toward the future, it is clear that a "baby boom echo" is building, creating national growth in the number of high school graduates. Meanwhile, our economy is generating demand for an increasingly skilled labor force. Colleges and school systems will need to intensify their efforts to work together. The students of the future will be more ethnically diverse, intensifying the imperative for us to eradicate the achievement gap among African American, Latino, Asian, and white students. Add to this a national teacher shortage that will affect schools and colleges alike, and it is clear that extraordinary challenges and some extraordinary opportunities lie ahead. Our capability for meeting these challenges will be determined in large measure by our capacity to work together regularly and effectively. School-college partnerships, K–16, need to be a priority for our educational organizations of the future.

Sharing resources and establishing common goals have begun to change the lives of students in Montgomery County. Boundaries between secondary and postsecondary curricula and instructional objectives have started to dissolve into a continuum of effort and progress that serves student needs before all else. The college is committed to partnership success. In the words of the president, "This is not only a partnership; it's a marriage." Superintendent Jerry Weast echoed this commitment: "The bar has been raised. The rest is up to all of us" (Weast, 1999).

References

Cross, K. P. *Opening Windows on Learning.* Mission Viego, California: League for Innovation in the Community College, 1998.

Larson, J. C., Garies, R., and Campbell, W. *A Profile of MCPS Graduates and their Performance at Montgomery College.* Rockville, Md.: Montgomery College/Montgomery County Public Schools, 1996.

Pew Charitable Trust. *The Bridge Project: Strengthening K-16 Transition Policies.* Stanford, Calif.: Stanford Institute on Higher Education Research, 1999.

Smith, T. M., and others. *The Condition of Education.* Washington D.C.: U.S. Department of Education, National Center for Education Statistics, 1997.

Weast, J. D. *A Call to Action: Raising the Bar.* Rockville, Md.: Montgomery County Public Schools, 1999.

CHARLENE R. NUNLEY is president of Montgomery College in Montgomery County, Maryland.

MARY KAY SHARTLE-GALOTTO is the provost of the Rockville Campus of Montgomery College.

MARY HELEN SMITH is the director of instruction for the Manassas City Public Schools, Manassas, Virginia.

8

Los Angeles Trade Technical College and the Los Angeles Unified School District have collaborated in several ways to help ethnically diverse, urban school children prepare for and make the transition to college.

Working with Urban Schools That Serve Predominantly Minority Students

May Kuang-chi Chen, James L. Konantz,
M. Lucia Rosenfeld, Clara Frost

Changing demographics have dramatically altered the makeup of the nation's student population. Increasing rates of poverty, divorce, single parenting, teen pregnancy, family mobility and instability, and employment outside the home of women with children have placed many students at risk of dropping out of school (U.S. Department of Education, 1997). "At the close of the twentieth century, higher education appears to be more important than ever—both to our economy and our competitive position in the world. . . .Yet large gaps persist, by income and race, in who benefits from higher education in the United States" (College Board, 2000, p. 2). Faced with mounting criticism about the decline of education in the United States, and particularly the failure to educate low-income and minority children, educators, political leaders, and community groups are fostering strategies for greater involvement. Among various intervention strategies, the middle college high school (MCHS) model, originally conceived by Janet Lieberman at LaGuardia Community College in New York City in 1974, has proven effective and has outlived many other models in the nation. (See Chapter Five in this volume.)

With the highest concentration of ethnic minorities, recent immigrants, and individuals with limited English proficiency, California has been facing similar concerns at a much higher level than has the nation as a whole. Both the concern and the strategy are well described in the California Community Colleges Board of Governors' *2005 Strategic Response* (1998): "Community colleges not only hold the key to success for millions of our citizens, but also the key to a workforce prepared to compete in a global economy, and the key to an educated citizenry that serves as the stable basis for a strong multi-cultural democracy" (p. 1). To achieve this potential, the board of governors has urged colleges to develop and implement a number of strategies, including improved articulation with high schools. This chapter describes the efforts of one California institution, Los Angeles Trade Technical College (LATTC, or Trade-Tech), to link with the schools in its urban, multicultural service area.

The Los Angeles Trade-Technical College Services Area

LATTC's service area embodies the issues outlined in the board of governors' report. Established in 1949, Trade-Tech offers degree and certificate programs in trade and technical subjects, as well as the associate degree for transfer to four-year colleges and universities. Most Trade-Tech students are the first in their families to enter any form of postsecondary education, and their success in college offers the possibility of economic and social accomplishment that their parents, often unskilled laborers, have been unable to achieve. Ethnic minorities represent the vast majority of the student body at Trade Tech. In fall 1999, the college's student population, totaling fifteen thousand, was composed of 10 percent Asian Americans, 30 percent African Americans, 52 percent Hispanics, and 7 percent whites and others, most of whom are recent immigrants from Russia and other Eastern European countries.

LATTC is located in south-central downtown Los Angeles, a neglected area with a high concentration of poverty. The service area of both Trade-Tech and its main feeder high schools is characterized by high unemployment, many single-parent families, and neighborhoods of ethnic minorities with high concentrations of limited English proficiency (LEP) populations and recent immigrants receiving welfare assistance. Other urban factors also present challenges to educators: a lack of neighborhood safety, stereotyping and discrimination, poor study habits and attitude, students' behavioral and psychological problems, as well as drugs and crime in student residential areas. Both the conditions of students' immediate living environment and the low level of their academic preparation place them in a disadvantaged status.

Collaborative Partnerships between Trade-Tech and Local High Schools

The educational needs in the locality and the problems that students face make it evident that more must be done to help local school children understand the importance of a college education. To plan, sustain, and continuously update and upgrade college-high school collaborations, project developers at Trade-Tech have been examining pertinent research findings and program evaluations. Meanwhile, popular program designs described in Lieberman (1988), Ignash (1997), Rosenbaum (1998), and other models suitable for an urban environment have also been studied. Over the years, LATTC and several high schools of the Los Angeles Unified School District (LAUSD), as well as a few private schools, have collaboratively initiated and implemented various research-supported, outcomes-based college-high school partnerships. These partnerships have the following main goals:

To prevent disadvantaged students from dropping out of high school by improving their academic performances and career opportunities

To improve the self-concept and self-esteem of disadvantaged students by providing them a supportive, academically challenging teaching and learning environment

To facilitate college attendance of low-achieving high school students who have high potential by offering them additional support from college faculty, staff, and student mentors

To enhance college and career options by exploring them with broad curricula that are academic and transfer oriented, as well as focused on workforce preparation

The target participants of these partnerships include those who, for a variety of reasons, may not be performing up to their full potential in a traditional school setting. However, all partners believe these students can reach a higher level by studying in a college setting that provides an atmosphere in which they can improve their academic performance, self-concept, and attendance and learn career options.

The Academic and Vocational Partnerships. In order to accomplish the fourfold goal and fulfill the varied educational needs of the huge disadvantaged student population in the area, Trade-Tech and its partners have initiated and sustained four major customized academic and vocational partnerships.

Full-Day Middle College High School Program. The Jefferson/Trade Tech Incentive High School, located on the Trade-Tech campus, has educated hundreds of students annually since 1993. Jefferson High School, the top Trade-Tech feeder school, initiated this program by renting classrooms and office space from Trade-Tech. Program participants are Jefferson students who have challenging circumstances in their lives, but are looking for a highly motivating and structured environment.

Participants are bused to Trade-Tech from Jefferson at 7:30 a.m. and leave the campus at 3:00 p.m. A free lunch program is available. In addition to receiving course credits in a college environment by taking both high school and college classes, participants receive personalized career and college counseling, as well as job placement and professional training opportunities. They enjoy all facilities available at Trade-Tech, including Olympic-size swimming pools, a college library, high-tech computer access, and a wide variety of academic and vocational courses. These resources may not otherwise be available to students on a traditional school campus.

Full-Day, Year-Round Center for Advanced Transition Skills. Nationwide in every community college service area, many high school students in special education programs may never attend college. After age eighteen, they may continue to enroll in high schools, become clients of social services agencies, or disappear to an unknown corner of the community.

Participants of the Center for Advanced Transition Skills have a more promising future. This program is designed to provide age-appropriate, work-based learning and career education to special education students who are eighteen to twenty-one years of age. LAUSD provides transportation, lunch, program insurance, a teacher, and two teacher's aides, and Trade-Tech hosts the center on campus.

Center participants must obtain high school teachers' recommendations and parental support, must meet California Department of Rehabilitation criteria, and must understand basic safety-related issues. They must also have destination travel experiences, the ability to stay on task for at least thirty minutes, and positive peer-adult relationships. The twelve participants are bused or come on public transportation every day from home to Trade-Tech, where they spend the entire day working and studying. Based on their interests and assessed abilities, participants take academic or vocational courses (or both) available on campus. In addition, they are assigned to various work sites on campus, including faculty and staff offices, the physical fitness center, the bookstore, and building and grounds areas. Under supervision of their mentors, participants develop career skills, become aware of potential career opportunities available in the community, and acquire skills necessary to make the transition to the post-high school community. The ultimate goal of this center is for participants to develop personal, community, and independent living skills.

Afternoon, Weekend College Program at Trade-Tech. Approximately two thousand students attend Trade-Tech prior to graduating from high school every year; among them are eight hundred concurrent high school students. Through Trade-Tech's Steps Ahead program, these students enroll in classes offered by Afternoon College or Saturday Academy. Students enrolled in these programs and courses fulfill high school graduation requirements, since some required courses are not offered at high schools; prepare for entry-level employment; earn college credit though advanced placement (AP) courses; earn a high school equivalency diploma (GED); or simply gain college experience.

Integrating multiculturalism and student support services into the classroom has been one of the important components of these programs and courses. Learning communities formed both inside and outside the classroom help students from varied backgrounds learn to work and socialize with each other. Meanwhile, student services and campus life are also brought into the classroom. Students are encouraged to take personal development courses (for example, on interpersonal relationships, career planning, or college success), which are transferable to the California State University System. These courses are designed to do the following:

Improve students' interpersonal skills and their understanding of people from different backgrounds
Enable students to make meaningful decisions regarding educational and career goals
Assist students in improving memory, time management, and study techniques, including note-taking and test-taking skills
Familiarize students with library utilization, financial aid application process and procedures, student services programs, and work opportunities on and off campus.

In addition, to ease students' transition to college and employment, Steps Ahead also enables the college to use its facility fully during the time blocks that otherwise would remain underused.

College Courses at High School Sites. Trade-Tech often offers customized programs and courses at high school sites. In general, high schools make these requests for three main reasons: they do not have teachers with the credentials or the facility to teach the subject; they would like to strengthen their students' skills in basic English and math, or workforce preparation; or they would like to provide a second chance for students who have failed the course previously. If it is only for the first reason, these courses can be offered anytime during the day. If it is for the latter two reasons, the courses are mostly offered after high school classes but before the adult school begins its classes. In urban areas, it is quite common that high school and adult school share the same facility.

Under this partnership, the high school's responsibility is to recruit students and determine the courses to be offered at the high school sites. Trade-Tech hires faculty members with appropriate experiences and credentials and selects textbooks and other instructional materials or equipment. Students may use the earned credits to fulfill high school graduation requirements or use them as college credits.

Program Effectiveness: Student Outcomes. Program effectiveness can be best presented by student outcomes. The following Jefferson/Trade-Tech Incentive High School's student outcome statistics demonstrate the program's success (LAUSD, 2000):

The number of Jefferson students concurrently attending full-day or afternoon programs at Trade-Tech has doubled from 150 to more than 300.
While 43 percent of all Trade-Tech students received a grade of C or better college grades, 82 percent of the Incentive High students did in 1998.

The average semester retention rate of Incentive High students, 90 percent, is fourteen percentage points higher than the average rate for Trade-Tech students.
In comparison with 59.6 percent of statewide college-going rate, the college-going rate of Incentive High School graduates is 100 percent.

As for the Center for Advanced Transition Skills, the success rate is 100 percent for the fall 1999 participants. Ten of the twelve participants continue to enroll in the program; two graduated from the program and enrolled as regular college students at Trade-Tech.

Outreach and College Introduction Activities

Trade-Tech has a set of comprehensive outreach and college introduction activities. From the School Relation Unit, professional staff and student ambassadors regularly visit local schools, as well as business and industries. Outreach activities include introducing specific academic and vocational programs on campus, displaying college information in high school display cases (for example, the names of graduates from the high school who have made the dean's list at Trade-Tech), and conducting early admissions application workshops and placement assessment. School relations professionals also provide general introductions about Trade-Tech: financial aid, the learning resource center, and other support services on campus. The college's Information Center is another important form of outreach, offering both a telephone hot line and walk-in service. Upon request, the center staff either mails information packages to potential students or directs them to the college home page. Information Center staff often host campus visits.

Other organized, routine activities include Tools for Success, a scholarship award sponsored by the Miller Brewing Company. This program provides actual tools and equipment for students who have been ignored by other scholarship programs and helps place the vocational graduates into the labor market through partnerships with local business and industry. Graduating students from Fashion Design, one of Trade-Tech's well-known programs, annually showcase their best designs at the Thimble Fashion Show, a fashion extravaganza that attracts numerous potential students from high schools and the community. Twice a year, Trade-Tech's Dance Ensemble, a dance concert put together and performed by faculty and students, draws a huge audience with interests in the performing arts and the entertainment business.

Recommendations

Among their multiple missions and roles, community colleges continue to serve as an important link between high schools and four-year higher education institutions or employers. As growing numbers of high school students emerge from nontraditional populations, community colleges must help to meet the their needs as they prepare for college education.

Educators at both Los Angeles Trade-Technical College and the Los Angeles Unified School District have had firsthand experiences in developing effective strategies to address these needs. This experience leads to several practical recommendations for community college administrators who seek to forge links with the school systems in their service areas.

Establish partnerships with total commitment, mutual understanding, and support. When establishing partnerships, all parties need to incorporate student success practices and procedures that have been developed through the college and the school district's self-assessment and strategic planning processes. When conflicts or problems occur, the partners need to communicate and reach a mutual agreement before advising the students. Meanwhile, the college faculty need to be fully informed about the program; some faculty may believe a college is for "college" students, not high school students.

Anticipate barriers, take one step at a time, and offer customized programs and courses. At the beginning, all partners should expect barriers; take small steps by offering customized, classroom-scale programs and courses; improve program and course design over time; and enjoy success one step at a time. Since each high school has unique needs, a one-size-fits-all approach will not work. The partners should not hesitate to discontinue a program if it is not working and then identify another model.

Help students with application and registration processes. High school participants can be overwhelmed by the paperwork and other processes needed to enroll in a college program. These students need a great deal of one-on-one guidance in order to complete the application process. Most have to be walked through the registration process more than once before completing it. Even then, there is no guarantee that they will complete the class. In order to increase the odds of the high school students' success, responsibility must be shared at both levels. There should be a forum for partners to discuss issues and concerns related to high school students' attending classes at the college. Such lateral communication increases awareness of how to serve the students better, and it increases understanding of respective needs and resources.

Conduct ongoing progress assessment and identify multiple success indicators. A major key to program success is not only to measure student outcomes, but also to assess project progress periodically, so that plans and strategies can be refined and improved throughout the duration of the project. The goal is to train faculty and staff to establish benchmarks for student success, conduct ongoing assessment, and follow up on the performance of all participants. Faculty members should also include classroom assessment techniques as instructional routines. Progress and success indicators may include course and service progress reports and completion and success rates; retention and persistence rates; program completion and success rates;

high school diploma or GED, and college certificate and/or associate degree receiving rates; transfer rates; and workforce employment rates.

Develop and implement a comprehensive counseling and tutoring plan. A comprehensive counseling and tutoring plan with implementation strategies and time lines should be developed and fully implemented. This plan may include professional counseling (group workshops and counseling, individual counseling sessions, and on-line counseling and information offering) and peer mentoring (academic tutoring, big brother or big sister mentoring, and student role models). It is more effective to identify counselors and tutors from multicultural and multilingual backgrounds to offer support services to students. In addition to group counseling and workshops on various topics, counselors advise students on a variety of areas, including class selection, career choices, and future planning. Furthermore, all project participants should have access to a wealth of additional support services from all other student services on campus, including the health center, counseling center, career placement center, and transfer center.

Address psychoemotional needs. All too often, urban factors have had a significantly negative impact on student learning, behaviors, attitudes, habits, value systems, and personality development. Skills and knowledge are only two of the essential elements students need for success in college and the rest of life. The psychoemotional and social resourcefulness of students in an urban environment also play a major role in their adjustment to the demands of college and life. In order to help students gain the personal strength and self-awareness that leads to this resourcefulness, we need to infuse psychoemotional education into the curriculum for precollege students. In addition to providing various personal development courses and counseling services, offering psychology and sociology courses could be another strategy.

Ensure state-of-the-art education delivery. State-of-the-art educational delivery methods may include up-to-date and upgraded curriculum design, integrated liberal arts and workforce education programs, innovative teaching and learning strategies, and cutting-edge technology. The partners need to examine and determine the sequencing and content level of all general education courses to be taught at both high school and college levels. In addition, institutional and classroom-based research should be applied to promote student success.

Fully institutionalize the project. To provide college experiences effectively to precollege program participants, community colleges should integrate these students fully into the college environment. This means that students should receive all educational and support services that are offered on campus. As a result, students will develop a real sense of belonging to the college. All partners should share with each other any new, innovative ideas in instructional delivery and student support services, as well as existing resources, including staff, equipment, and facilities.

Form consortia to seek further financial resources. The roots of unequal educational opportunity are deep. Educational needs of students in an urban environment are significant. Fortunately, many funding agencies at local, state, and national levels are familiar with and sympathetic to these needs. Various federal grants are specifically designed for the needy students, among them, Upward Bound, Talent Search, TRIO, and GEAR-UP. When all partners feel that they are ready to institutionalize the school-to-college collaboration fully and sustain systematic changes, they should seek additional financial support. For example, the LATTC/LAUSD Consortium has recently received a five-year grant from the Chancellor's Office of California Community Colleges to found a comprehensive MCHS program on the Trade-Tech campus. This means, over the coming five-year period, that an additional three hundred high school students will be able to enjoy the afternoon and weekend college programs in both fall and spring semesters, and the full-day program during the summer session each year. Furthermore, the Advanced Transitional Center will serve twenty-four participants, twice the current size. To strengthen this collaboration, community college and high school partners should not hesitate to seek additional financial support from outside resources.

Conclusion

All of the recommendations provided point to the conclusion that urban community colleges are indelibly linked to the schools from which their students come. If the seeds of student success in college are sown well before high school graduation, then the college cannot relinquish its obligation to help students before they graduate from high school. In the end, serving ethnically diverse populations living on the margins of American society is a joint college-school responsibility that entails attention to the academic, economic, social, and psychological factors that have an impact on the upward academic mobility of urban students.

References

California Community Colleges Board of Governors. *2005 Strategic Response*. Sacramento: California Community Colleges Board of Governors, 1998.

College Board. *ConnectED 2000, Engaging a Nation*. New York: College Board, 2000.

Ignash, J. M. (ed.). *Implementing Effective Policies for Remedial and Developmental Education*. New Directions for Community Colleges, no. 100. San Francisco: Jossey-Bass, 1997.

Lieberman, J. E. (ed.). *Collaborating with High Schools*. New Directions for Community Colleges, no. 63. San Francisco: Jossey-Bass, 1988.

Los Angeles Community College District. *Annual Information Digest*. Los Angeles: Office of Research, Los Angeles Community College District, 1999.

Los Angeles Unified School District. *Program Review: Thomas Jefferson High School Los Angeles Trade-Technical College Incentive Program*. Los Angeles: Los Angeles Unified School District, 2000.

Rosenbaum, K. *Unrealistic Plans and Misdirected Efforts: Are Community Colleges Getting the Right Message to High School Students?* New York: Columbia University, Teachers College, 1998.

U.S. Department of Education. *For People Concerned About Education*. Washington, D.C.: U.S. Department of Education, 1997.

MAY KUANG-CHI CHEN is dean of enrollment management, Los Angeles Trade-Technical College.

JAMES L. KONANTZ is director of the instructional technology branch of the Los Angeles Unified School District.

M. LUCIA ROSENFELD is the administrator of the office of career and transition services instructional technology branch of the Los Angeles Unified School District.

CLARA FROST is student recruitment coordinator, Los Angeles Trade-Technical College.

9

Legal problems can emerge when high school students enroll in college courses or when college staff work within the schools. This chapter discusses potential legal problems and offers strategies for addressing them.

Anticipating Legal Problems When Working with High School Students

Elizabeth T. Lugg

As high school curricula become more diverse and competitive, and funding and resources become less abundant, many school districts are turning to area community colleges as an alternative for students who are seeking advanced courses. By having junior and senior high school students attend classes at the community college, the local high school is able to broaden and enrich its curriculum without hiring additional staff or finding additional teaching space. This type of partnership, however, increases the legal liability of both the local school district and the community college. Once minor students are mixed with adult students in an adult setting—the community college campus—the possibility for a controversial incident rises dramatically. This is not because the community college campus is inherently more dangerous, but rather because a different standard of care is expected of educators who deal with high school rather than community college students. This different standard of care would also be experienced by community college staff who come into the high school to assist in providing instruction. Once in the high school, the community college employee is held to the same standard of care as the high school teacher. To understand what is meant by standard of care, a short refresher on tort law is necessary.

A Primer on Basic Tort Law

American civil law covers instances where one private individual, or group of individuals, commits a wrong or an injury against another private individual or group of individuals. The remedy provided in civil cases is monetary damages. Torts are a category of these civil wrongs. Negligence torts are of particular interest to educators participating in K–12 collaborations with community colleges.

Reasonable Person. The tort theory of negligence is the one most often encountered in the school setting. It revolves around the idea of the "reasonable person." In a very basic sense, it is the failure of an individual to behave and use the standard of care that a reasonable person of like characteristics would use under similar circumstances. "Like characteristics" refers to the physical characteristics of the defendant—size, weight, physical abilities—and not the mental characteristics or experience. The theory of negligence is very fact specific; the results of any one lawsuit are dependent on the specific facts before the court. Those facts, however, are fit into a template to help with the decision. For a plaintiff to be successful in a negligence lawsuit, he or she must show the following:

- A duty of care existed between the defendant and the plaintiff.
- The defendant failed to provide the standard of care required by the situation.
- This failure to exercise the proper standard of care was the actual and proximate cause of the plaintiff's injury.
- There were actual damages to the plaintiff.

Duty of Care. When talking about the educational setting, there is little doubt that the group of individuals most likely to become defendants— teachers, staff, and volunteers—clearly owe a duty of care to the students whom they supervise. The duty of care is easily foreseeable. What differs between the duty of care owed a high school student and the duty of care owed a community college student is the concept of in loco parentis.

In Loco Parentis. In loco parentis, which means "to stand in the place of the parent," is a legal concept applied to K–12 education. In the context of the high school, it allows faculty and staff to assume the status of the high school student's parents. Traditionally this doctrine has been used to insulate teachers from criticism for their discipline of students. In current practice, however, the doctrine of in loco parentis is used for both disciplinary and nondisciplinary situations to establish the duty and standard of care owed to the student by the educator.

The courts have generally held that in loco parentis does not apply to colleges and universities. In today's society, higher education institutions are viewed as educational rather than custodial institutions, thereby diminishing the duty and standard of care that the employees of the college or university owe to their students. The one exception that courts have noted, however, is when a college or university chooses to have minor children live on campus during a summer camp or academic program, because then the higher education institution is again viewed as a custodial institution standing in loco parentis (*University of Denver v. Whitlock,* 1987; *Rabel v. Illinois Wes-*

leyan University, 1987; *Nero v. Kansas State University,* 1993; *Fox v. Board of Supervisors of Louisiana State University,* 1991).

A similar situation occurs when high school students are on community college campuses. When high school students are at the high school, their parents have a reasonable expectation that the students will be looked after in the same manner as if they were with their parents. In other words, the parents can reasonably believe that from the time they drop their children off at the school (or the school bus stop) until that student reappears at the end of the day, the children will be supervised and protected so that no harm will befall them. There is no similar expectation by the parents of community college students, and therefore many community colleges have not set up the elaborate supervisory plans that are commonplace in high schools. The question then becomes, Which standard is to be used when high school students are on community college campuses?

Standard of Care. Once it has been settled that there is a duty of care, the next question is what standard defines that duty. This is where the reasonable person standard comes in. For everyone, there is a legal duty to act as a reasonable person of like characteristics would under similar circumstances. For an educator, this automatically includes a duty to supervise and instruct properly. When dealing with high school students, this standard of care is greater than what is expected when dealing with adult students in a community college. The standard of care for a teacher of high school students is going to be dictated by the age and maturity of the students. High school students are still minors. In the eyes of the court, they still lack the ability and maturity to behave as adults. This is the reason they are unable to do such things as enter into contracts, drink alcohol, smoke cigarettes, be drafted, or marry without the consent of a parent. Community college students are, for the most part, eighteen years old or older. The courts view them as adults, with all the rights and responsibilities of adults, including the expectation that they will behave in a reasonable manner.

Community college staff, when dealing with their adult students, owe the standard of care of one individual instructing another individual. When those community college staff are interacting with or instructing high school students, the standard of care—what is considered reasonable behavior—changes. If the community college and the high school are operating under an agreement of some sort, the parent of the high school student may reasonably expect that the staff of the community college will exercise the same care in ensuring that his or her child is safe as is exercised by employees of the local high school. Should harm occur to the child, that parent has standing to sue both the local school district and the community college.

The duty to supervise is the most common cause of tort litigation against schools, both K–12 and higher education. The courts have held that teachers have the duty to supervise and instruct students during the school day when those students are on school property or at a school-sponsored event off school property. Some courts have even stretched this duty to include supervision when the student is on school property regardless of whether it is during the school day or at a school-sponsored event. Once the teacher is aware that the student is on school property, even after school hours, the teacher assumes the duty to supervise that student (*Versprill v. School Board of Orange County,* 1994).

Moreover, the court in *Brownell v. Los Angeles Unified School District* (1992) reaffirmed that the duty to supervise typically ends when the students leave the school grounds at the end of the day, unless the school has assumed greater responsibility. This concept bears directly on the concept of high school students taking classes at a community college. If this is done through a partnership between the school district and the community college, it could be argued that the school district has assumed greater liability. If, however, the student is taking classes at the community college on his or her own time and not under an arrangement with the local school district, the question of duty to supervise shifts under the decision in *Brownell.*

Another case, *Palella v. Ulmer* (1987), states that the duty to supervise may extend beyond the normal school day. As long as it can be said that the school has custody of the child, the duty to exercise reasonable care exists. Again, this could mean that the local school is the one responsible for the child even when he or she is attending classes at a community college—or it may imply just the opposite.

Defenses to Claims of Negligence

State educational institutions, whether K–12 or higher education, enjoy some defenses against the charge of negligence, not the least of which is the concept of sovereign immunity.

Sovereign Immunity. The concept of sovereign immunity is a legal doctrine dating back to English law. Another name for sovereign immunity is *governmental immunity.* What the concept means is that, as a general rule, federal, state, and local governments and their political subdivisions are immune from tort liability. It goes back to the idea that a British subject cannot sue the king of England. Over the years in the United States, however, much of this immunity has been dissolved through state statutes, constitutional provisions, or case law. Today most school districts still enjoy immunity from tort litigation unless it can be shown that a representative of the school district either acted outside of his or her employment or behaved in such an egregious manner that the conduct was willful, wanton, reckless, or in bad faith and therefore was not immune.

The rationale behind providing immunity to the government, including schools and school personnel, is to give those individuals ultimate latitude in dealing with the day-to-day operations of the school. This seems to be keeping in order with the concept of in loco parentis. Parents and guardians enjoy such immunity and, thus, so should school personnel when they are standing in the place of the parents. The other rationale stems from the belief that private litigation against a public school is coun-terproductive to society. After all, any monetary award is really paid for by the citizens of the district through tax dollars. It is better for those resources to be used for the education of children than to defend against tort litigation. Therefore, only the most blatant conduct is actionable.

Assumption of Risk. Another defense to tort liability that applies quite well to the educational setting is assumption of risk. This legal doctrine holds that an individual cannot be guilty of negligence for an activity that is known to be potentially dangerous if the individuals participating have been noti-fied of the risk and have agreed to participate anyway. If a school wishes to use assumption of risk as a defense, three elements must be shown:

1. The injured party knew that the activity was dangerous.
2. The injured party understood the risk involved in the activity.
3. The injured party voluntarily agreed to participate in the activity even after knowing about and understanding the risk.

In school cases this defense is most often used in incidents dealing with sports.

Addressing the Potential Increase in Liability

Legal liability is most likely to increase when a community college decides to partner with a high school to offer upper-level courses that involve person-to-person contact, including student-to-student and teacher-to-student con-tact. There would not be a significant increase in risk when talking about transportation or curriculum per se. Risk would arise only in these areas when interpersonal communication was involved (such as altercations between stu-dents in the parking lot or at the bus stop or a method of instruction used by an instructor). There are measures that both the high school and the com-munity college can take in order to decrease the likelihood that anything neg-ative might happen.

A partnership agreement is the one document that should be indis-pensable to both community colleges and public schools when high school students will be attending classes on the community college campus. This document provides evidence of an explicit assumption of risk by both the student and the student's parents. Following is a checklist regarding such a partnership agreement:

Collaborate with local school districts to devise the form. Include specific language about the adult atmosphere on the community college campus, including the lessened supervision. Put students and parents on notice that it is not reasonable for them to have the same expectations regarding supervision and standard of care that they have when the student in on the high school campus.

Require all minor students and their parents to sign the agreement before the student's registration is complete. If both do not sign the agreement, the student will not be allowed to attend classes.

Have the students and their parents sign a new agreement form each registration period. Do not assume that one form will suffice for the entire time in which the high school student may be in attendance. By having the form signed every semester, the student and his or her parents are constantly on notice regarding any risk. The community college has thus proven the first element: that the student and parent know the risks associated with the minor student's attendance on the community college campus.

Provide on the form the name, address, and telephone number of an individual at the community college who can be contacted if the student or parent has any questions about or difficulty in understanding the agreement. Wording near the signatory line should state that the signature indicates that the student and parent have read and understood the agreement and voluntarily agree to participate in the activity. This will ensure that the student or parent cannot later claim that they did not understand the risk. This is also the reason to have the parent as well as the student sign. Sometimes the age of an individual will determine whether he or she can actually assume risk. Therefore, because the student is a minor, it is unwise to have the agreement signed only by him or her.

Sexual Harassment Policy and Procedure

The other major area of liability in a high school–community college partnership is in the area of sexual harassment, both teacher to student and student to student. The likelihood that sexual harassment will occur should decrease if the school takes the following steps:

Has a comprehensive policy for both faculty and students expressing zero tolerance for sexual harassment

Distributes the policy regularly

Provides in-service training to faculty, staff, students, and parents regarding sexual harassment and appropriate behavior

Has an investigative procedure in place and responds immediately and consistently to any reports of incidents of harassment

Has a consistent and documented discipline procedure for offenders

In-Service Training for Staff on the Concepts of Harassment and Appropriate Behavior with Minor Students. Although the partnership agreement is the best method for dealing with increased tort liability when the high school student is on the community college campus, intensive in-service training for community college faculty and staff should be effective to decrease liability when the high school student is on campus and the community college employee goes into the high school. Following are some topics that might be dealt with during in-service training:

Elements of sexual harassment, including quid pro quo and hostile environment.
Quid pro quo harassment is what people typically think of when they discuss
sexual harassment. Examples include a student who is forced to comply with
the sexual demands of a teacher to receive a passing grade. In student-against-
student harassment, an example might be one or more students' forcing sexual actions on another student in the locker room after gym class or an athletic
practice. A single episode is usually sufficient to trigger liability. Hostile environment sexual harassment, on the other hand, is defined as conduct of a sexual nature that makes the recipient feel uncomfortable—for example, lewd and
vulgar suggestions and comments, pornographic pictures, and whistling, star-
ing, and treating individuals differently because of their gender. What may
appear to be mere vulgar horseplay can, in fact, be harassment if the targeted
individual feels threatened or intimidated. Hostile environment harassment
can also involve the use of nonsexual jokes, pranks, and even assaults. Unlike
quid pro quo harassment, hostile environment harassment must be pervasive.
An isolated offensive act is insufficient grounds for holding an institution liable.
Moreover, when dealing with minor students, there is always the overlay of
criminal charges for inappropriate sexual acts with a minor, which may make
the civil penalties for sexual harassment pale in comparison.

*A discussion of recent court rulings dealing with teacher-to-student and student-
to-student harassment.*

The laws under which an individual can be convicted of sexual harassment. In
the context of minor students, this would include not only the civil penalties for sexual harassment but also the criminal penalties, including felony-
level penalties, and the ramifications that such criminal actions have on the
career of those found guilty.

*A discussion of what is considered appropriate behavior with a student, espe-
cially a minor student.* The discussion should encompass that teacher-student
relationships, when the student is a minor, are never consensual and therefore are forbidden. Another topic is that students are to treat all other students with courtesy and respect.

*For faculty and staff, strategies to be used to avoid even the appearance of
impropriety.* Examples are never meeting with a student behind closed doors,
never meeting with a student at local eateries or drinking establishments,
and avoiding physical contact.

*A review and explanation of the institution's sexual harassment policy, investi-
gatory procedures, and resulting discipline.*

Complete and Detailed Policies for Dealing with Student Conduct.
This proactive stance should start with the establishment of a clear-cut policy against sexual harassment of employees and students. This policy, while
not rising to an affirmative defense that can completely obviate all employer
or institutional responsibility, at the very least will provide a mitigating factor in any sort of litigation. It has been shown that schools, both K–12 and
higher educational institutions, that do not have a policy prohibiting sexual
harassment are more likely to be held liable than those that do.

Conclusion

Allowing high school students the opportunity to further their education by taking courses at a local community college is a concept that should benefit all involved. Unfortunately, the minute that adult learners are mixed with minor students in a fairly unsupervised setting, the chance increases for something to happen that may open either educational institution—the local school district or the community college—to excessive legal liability. The legal liability referred to in this instance is a claim of negligence regarding the behavior of the educational institution.

Although allegations are easily dealt with through one or more legal defenses, the standard of care owed a minor high school student by his or her teacher differs from the standard of care owed an adult learner by his or her teacher. High school faculty stand in loco parentis toward their students, while community college faculty do not—unless that community college faculty member chooses to enter the high school to conduct courses. Once the players involved understand the difference in the standard of care, simple preplanning can diminish or even extinguish some of the excessive legal liability. The area where problems are most likely to occur are any interpersonal contact among faculty, staff, and students. The two examples are curricular content and sexual harassment, either teacher-to-student or student-to-student. Questionable curricular content can be dealt with prior to students' enrollment by providing notice of the content of the course and giving each student and his or her parents the final choice as to whether to register anyway. As for sexual harassment, the educational institution can lessen its legal liability if it has a comprehensive policy addressing sexual harassment, disseminates that policy, and educates faculty, staff, students, and parents on the topic of sexual harassment.

Insisting that the minor high school student and his or her parents sign a partnership agreement is the most effective method of reducing excess legal liability. With this document, the community college and the local high school have allowed the student and parent to assume the increased risk of the high school student's attending classes on the community college campus. The partnership agreement puts the student and parent on notice that there are increased risks (such as less intensive supervision) on a community college campus, explains those risks, and gives the student and parent the choice as to whether they wish to participate in the program regardless of the increased risk.

References

Brownell v. Los Angeles Unified School District, 5 Cal. Rptr. 2d 756 (Cal. Ct. App. 1992).
Fox v. Board of Supervisors of Louisiana State University, 576 So.2d 978 (La. 1991).
Nero v. Kansas State University, 861 P.2d 768 (Kan. 1993).
Palella v. Ulmer, 518 N.Y.S.2d 91 (N.Y. Sup. Ct. 1987).
Rabel v. Illinois Wesleyan University, 514 N.E.2d 552 (Ill. App. Ct. 1987).

University of Denver v. Whitlock, 744 P.2d 54 (Colo. 1987).

Versprill v. School Board of Orange County, 641 So. 2d 883 (Fla. Dist. Ct. app. 1994).

ELIZABETH T. LUGG *is an attorney at law and an assistant professor of educational administration and foundations at Illinois State University.*

10

The significant number of recent high school graduates who move on to the community college, as well as state education reform policies that link student achievement in school to subsequent success in college, require community colleges to monitor student flow from the high schools and articulate curricula with the courses offered in local school districts.

Demographics, State Education Reform Policies, and the Enduring Community College Role as an Extension of the Schools

James C. Palmer

Over the decades, community college leaders and advocates have championed the institution as a cure for large social problems. Their pronouncements mirror the ideals or fears of the times, not to mention ever-shifting legislative agendas. For example, in 1947, the President's Commission on Higher Education saw the community college as a democratizing agent, preparing the educated citizenry needed by a world power. Later, community college leaders posited their institutions as centers for community development and renewal (Gleazer, 1980; Pifer, 1974). More recently, the focus has been on economic development and workforce training (Zeiss, 1997).

But throughout, the community college has remained constant in one important way: it continues to provide instruction at the thirteenth- and fourteenth-grade levels to the citizens of defined, local communities. It therefore acts as the neighborhood school of American higher education, extending the reach of local school districts and connecting them to state university systems. This is what the community college uniquely does. A host of institutions and agencies provides job training and ad hoc adult education. Many other colleges and universities provide undergraduate education to individuals screened through an admissions process. But no other institution has the task of bringing the first two years of college to all citizens of local communities.

Demographics and policy ensure the continued predominance of this educational role within the community college mission. The gradually

NEW DIRECTIONS FOR COMMUNITY COLLEGES, no. 111, Fall 2000 © Jossey-Bass, a Wiley company

increasing number of young people emerging from the schools coincides with state school reform policies that emphasize student attainment of defined outcomes at each grade level and that view colleges as part of the larger K–16 system. There are at least two implications for cooperative work between community colleges and high schools. The first lies in the need to monitor student flow from high school to college. The second lies in the expectation that colleges and schools will provide these students with an articulated educational pathway that minimizes course duplication and documents achievement along the way.

Student Movement from High School to College

The steady flow of students from the schools to the community colleges ensures a de facto interdependency between the two sectors. Data reported by Kojaku and Nuñez (1999) reveal that of the students who entered college for the first time during 1995–96, 46 percent began their postsecondary studies at a public two-year institution. Looking only at numbers for public two-year and four-year colleges puts community college work with recent high school graduates in a keener perspective. Of all the first-time college students who enrolled in public two-year or four-year institutions during 1995–96 within one year of their high school graduation, 54 percent did so at a community college, and the remaining 46 percent enrolled in public four-year colleges. Of all those first-time enrollees at public two-year and four-year colleges who were under the age of twenty-four, 59 percent were at community colleges and 41 percent were at four-year colleges (Kojaku and Nuñez, 1999). Within the public sector of higher education, the community colleges are clearly a predominant destination for college-bound high school seniors.

Enrollment data from the 1990s, as well as demographic projections into the future, suggest that the number of young students entering community colleges will rise. From 1993 to 1997 (the last year for which published national enrollment data are available on the age distribution of college students), public two-year colleges experienced enrollment growth at both ends of the age continuum (see Table 10.1). Enrollments increased for two groups of students: those under the age of twenty-three, especially those who are age seventeen or younger (a group that likely includes high school students who are enrolling concurrently in college classes), and those who were age forty or older. In contrast, the number of students between the ages of twenty-three and forty declined. Demographic trends indicate that the group of students who are twenty-three or younger will continue to grow. The U.S. Department of Education estimates that because of the growing number of eighteen year olds in the nation's population, the number of high school graduates in 2009 will be 23 percent higher than the number of people who graduated from high school in 1997 (Gerald and Hussar, 1999). Accordingly, the department's midrange

Table 10.1. Percentage Change in Enrollment in Public Two-Year Colleges, by Age, 1993–1997

Age	1993			1997			Percentage Change from 1993 to 1997		
	Total	Full Time	Part Time	Total	Full Time	Part Time	Total	Full Time	Part Time
Under 18	129,781	32,868	96,913	211,071	41,392	169,679	63	26	75
18 and 19	969,320	653,654	315,666	1,041,984	704,001	337,983	7	8	7
20 and 21	784,133	399,388	384,745	820,262	423,511	396,751	5	6	3
22–24	753,225	258,050	495,175	688,382	233,451	454,931	–9	–10	–8
25–29	760,879	194,690	566,189	745,937	188,102	557,835	–2	–3	–1
30–34	608,741	130,720	478,021	511,795	102,674	409,121	–16	–21	–14
35–39	484,104	91,569	392,535	435,016	75,845	359,171	–10	–17	–8
40–49	552,998	89,835	463,163	572,028	84,775	487,253	3	–6	5
50–64	184,128	20,062	164,066	218,270	21,871	196,399	19	9	20
65 or over	55,154	3,067	52,087	60,490	2,560	57,930	10	–17	11
Age unknown	54,865	14,604	40,261	55,451	12,845	42,606	1	–12	6
Total	5,337,328	1,888,507	3,448,821	5,360,686	1,891,027	3,469,659	0	0	1

Source: Snyder and Hoffman (2000); Snyder, Hoffman, and Geddes (1996).

projections between 1997 and 2009 portray a shift in the age range of the college student population: "The increases in the younger population are expected to offset the loss of students from the older population, thereby contributing to the increases in college enrollment over the projected period" (Gerald and Hussar, 1999, p. 11).

These national averages mask considerable variations by region and state. Projections indicate that eight states will experience declines in the number of high school graduates through 2009 (relative to 1996), while increases registered in the remaining states will range from 1 percent to 103 percent; the median increase will be 13 percent (see Table 10.2). Yet the overall trend is clear: the community college role as an extension of the schools will remain an important part of the institution's mission. Monitoring and facilitating student flow from school districts to community colleges will remain an important objective of school-college collaboration.

Table 10.2. Projected Percentage Increase in the Number of Students Graduating from High School, by State, 1996–97 to 2008–9

State	Percentage Change	State	Percentage Change
Nevada	103	Pennsylvania	12
Arizona	76	Mississippi	11
North Carolina	48	Minnesota	11
Florida	45	Idaho	11
California	41	Oklahoma	10
Illinois	38	Vermont	9
Georgia	36	Indiana	9
Colorado	31	Wisconsin	8
Texas	30	South Carolina	7
Massachusetts	29	Kansas	5
Connecticut	28	Ohio	5
Hawaii	28	Nebraska	4
Maryland	25	Alabama	4
Washington	25	Mississippi	3
New Jersey	23	Utah	3
New Hampshire	22	Kentucky	1
New York	21	Iowa	0
Delaware	21	Montana	–1
Tennessee	20	Maine	–3
Virginia	20	South Dakota	–3
New Mexico	20	Washington, D.C.	–5
Oregon	17	Louisiana	–5
Arkansas	16	West Virginia	–7
Michigan	14	North Dakota	–8
Rhode Island	13	Wyoming	–15
Arkansas	13		

Source: Gerald and Hassar (1999).

Community colleges have approached this work in at least two ways. One is an institutional research approach in which colleges or college systems track the proportion of recent high school graduates who continue their education at two-year institutions; results can be used internally and shared with school administrators. Examples in the published literature include state-level analyses in Florida (Windham, 1996), Oklahoma (Oklahoma State Regents for Higher Education, 1997), and Oregon (Oregon University System, 1998). Examples of institutionally specific studies include those produced by Miami-Dade Community College (Baldwin, 1998; Morris, 1998) and the City College of San Francisco (1999). All provide empirical pictures of the magnitude of student flow from local schools to local colleges. For example, Morris (1998) found that of the Dade County Public High School graduates who enrolled in college during 1996–1997, 65 percent enrolled at Miami-Dade Community College. In contrast, the City College of San Francisco (1999) found that it enrolled only 24 percent of the 1997 graduates from public San Francisco high schools.

The second approach entails institutional marketing. In this approach, schools cooperate with two-year colleges to survey high school students about their future educational plans, their institutional preferences for college, and their impressions of the local community college. Findings provide insights into which students are more likely to attend community colleges, which aspects of the colleges appeal to students, and which aspects do not. For example, South Carolina's Spartanburg Technical College (STC) surveyed 1,501 juniors in fourteen surrounding high schools. Findings revealed that 36 percent of the juniors were considering a community technical college and 29 percent were considering attendance at STC (Quinley and Cantrell, 1998). The study also determined how students had learned about STC and that the students were more positive about STC as a "good place to study and earn a degree" than they were about STC's student organizations and activities, the ease with which students can get help with problems, the degree to which students from diverse backgrounds get along at STC, and the degree to which STC "is a college students are proud to attend" (Quinley and Cantrell, 1998, p. 7). The latter findings suggest a need to attend to the expectations that younger, full-time students have for full involvement in campus life, expectations that may be at odds with an institutional focus on convenience for older, part-time learners.

School Reform Policy

State school reform policies affecting the education of young people emerging from the schools also reinforce the importance of school-college connections. In an era in which most students (67 percent) go on to college within twelve months of high school graduation (U.S. Bureau of the Census, 1999) and in which college is viewed as a requisite for viable employment, it becomes harder for college leaders to disassociate themselves from school improvement efforts. Many state policymakers have made this clear through a K–16 orientation that posits schools and colleges as part of a seamless educational system. (See, for example, Langenberg, 1998; Tafel and Eberhart, 1999.) The unifying rhetoric of the K–16 movement has been coupled with an emphasis on standards-based testing in the schools, tying student progression from one grade level to the next with demonstrated mastery of specific skills or knowledge. (See Finn and Petrilli, 2000, for a review of these standards.) The result is closer scrutiny of curriculum articulation between the secondary and postsecondary sectors. Invoking both efficiency and equity, policymakers aim for a reduction in the need for remedial programs at college. They also seek an increase in the college-going rates of minority and low-income students (Langenberg, 1998; Chenoweth, 2000).

Oregon offers a prominent example. Its standards-based school reform efforts have been tied to college admissions at both the university and the community college. For example, the Oregon University System (2000a, 2000b) is currently phasing in the Proficiency-based Admissions Standards System (PASS) that makes admission to the state's public universities dependent, in part, on student mastery of learning standards that represent expectations for student achievement in high school. The goal has been to "ensure that the PASS proficiencies and their criteria align closely with the content standards and benchmarks for the Certificates of Initial and Advanced Mastery (CIM and CAM) that students earn" through assessments at the 10th and 12th grades, respectively (Oregon University System, 2000a). A parallel effort has been undertaken by the state's community colleges, which are developing "proficiency statements [that] . . . inform students of the knowledge and skills they are expected to have upon entry into individual college programs if they are to complete the program within its stipulated length" (Oregon Department of Community Colleges and Workforce Development, 1999). These statements, aligned with both the CIM and CAM testing programs, list state standards for learning and note the extent to which each is "needed for entry" or "helpful to success" in specific occupational programs. (Exhibit 10.1 provides an example, linking state standards for speech communication to the proficiencies needed for success in an associate of applied science degree in criminal justice at Clackamas Community College.) Both the PASS program and the proficiency statements developed by the community college represent an attempt to make student progression from school to college contingent on actual learning, not just on student transcripts. "A proficiency-based system moves the focus of the admission process from courses taken to knowledge and skills mastered, linking admission directly to a student's demonstrated ability to meet clear performance standards" (Oregon University System, 2000b).

Concern for student achievement in articulated K–16 systems has also led to the development of regional and local educational consortia that link otherwise disparate educational bureaucracies. These consortia involve

Exhibit 10.1 Speech Communications Proficiency Statements for the Associate in Applied Science Degree Program in Criminal Justice, Clackamas Community College (OR)

Extended Definition: Speech Communication includes the skills of both listening and speaking. The competent communicator asks clarifying and extended questions, can distinguish between inferences and facts, is able to initiate and sustain conversations, discloses feelings and emotions, actively listens to ideas and opinions, and can give and receive directions clearly and accurately. Competent communication encompasses both verbal and nonverbal behaviors, and the ability to recognize that both carry social and personal meanings.

Proficiencies	Needed for Entry	Helpful to Success
1. Explain the importance of speaking and listening, and the respective roles and responsibilities of being a speaker and a listener.	X	
2. Ask and appropriately respond to closed or open questions.		X
3. Differentiate among facts, opinion, conclusions, and feelings.		X
4. Engage in small talk as a means for effective communication.		X
5. Disclose appropriately their own emotions and empathize with the emotions of others.		
6. Organize ideas in a logical sequence and present a clear, focused message.		
7. Follow oral directions accurately.	X	
8. Understand how nonverbal messages can enhance or detract from verbal messages.		
9. Identify the diversity of communication styles due to cultural differences.		

Source: Oregon Department of Community Colleges and Workforce Development (2000). (Source: http://www.odccwd.state.or.us/comcol/CH00/Chemekta%20Criminal.htm). This is a sample for only one competency. *Note:* Additional statements are listed for reading, writing, second languages, health and human performance, humanities and literature, mathematics, science, and social sciences. Technical competencies, developed by the college itself, are also listed.

community colleges, universities, and the schools in concerted efforts to promote student progress from grade to grade and from school to college. For example, P–16 councils (that is, preschool to grade 16) have been established in Georgia, consisting of "P–12 and postsecondary educators, school board members, youth advocate organizations, community members, and legislative and business leaders [who] have voluntarily formed to 'promote' and 'recommend' changes [that will] . . . improve student success at all levels" (Tafel and Eberhart, 1999, p. 10). Some of the councils are developing standards that define "what students should know and be able to do to be admitted to college, technical institute, or to enter the workforce." They are also developing standards that "define what students should know and be able to do upon completion of general education in college" (Tafel and Eberhart, 1999, p. 10). Similar collaborative efforts to articulate schooling and postsecondary education in other locations are described by Navarro and Natalicio (1999) and by McGrath and Van Buskirk (1999).

Both the newly formed admissions policies in Oregon and the emerging educational consortia underscore the ambitious expectation that the entire undergraduate curriculum will complement the work of the schools. High school connections with the colleges are to extend beyond targeted initiatives such as tech-prep programs for high school students pursuing specific careers (see Chapter Three), concurrent enrollment opportunities that allow high school students to take college courses (see Chapter Four), or the joint college-school sponsorship of summer career academies funded by federal school-to-work legislation (Merren, Hefty, and Soto, 1997). In the wake of the school and K–16 reform movements, the targeted, programmatic approach to work with the schools gives way to an institutional approach in which curriculum is viewed as a shared responsibility of educators at schools and neighboring colleges. Just as community college educators have been called on to facilitate transfer through joint curricular work with universities, and not simply through the services of transfer centers or other discrete units in the college (Eaton and others, 1988), so too have the colleges been called on to act cooperatively with the schools.

Joint school-college efforts described in the literature also beg the question of assessment. Besides monitoring student flow from the secondary to the postsecondary sectors, colleges and schools face the challenge of understanding the relationship between the student experience in high school and subsequent success in college. Research conducted at Frederick Community College (FCC) in Maryland provides an example, correlating retention and other measures of student progress at FCC with the types of courses students take while in high school (Holton, 1998a, 1998b). Another example stems from a survey of area high school students conducted by Johnson County Community College (JCCC) in Kansas. Among other findings, the survey data revealed a discrepancy between student aspirations and student plans for subsequent study: "85 percent of the respondents . . . planned to earn a bachelor's degree or higher, yet only 57 percent were following a college preparatory course of study" (Conklin, 1996, p. 80). The data also revealed that the students underestimate their need for remediation. Both the FCC and JCCC studies illustrate the type of research that will help colleges assess the results of their collaborative work with schools.

Conclusion

It is useful to underscore the factors that compel community college attention to the schools. They emphasize the fact that community colleges are not free agents. The continuing stream of students emerging from the schools, along with policies that reflect the enduring American expectation that young people will have an opportunity to attend college, exerts a powerful influence on community colleges, as do the requirements of universities to which many community college students transfer. Despite the expansion of the curriculum implied in the transformation from junior to community college after World War II, providing instruction at the thirteenth- and fourteenth-grade levels for recent high school graduates remains central to the mission. In one fundamental sense, today's two-year colleges are what they always have been: institutions standing between the schools and the universities.

It is for this reason that calls for a radical transformation of the community college rarely take hold. Calls made by Pifer (1974), Gleazer (1980), and others in the 1960s and 1970s to view the institution more as a community service agency than as a college reflected admirable ideals for social improvement, but they ran counter to the public's demand for traditional schooling. So too may contemporary visions of transformed community colleges. For example, the "learning college" proposed by O'Banion (1997) appeals to the ideals of lifelong learning and student-centered instruction. But its approach to curriculum as a variable construct that is individually tailored for each student conflicts with the directive role of the community college as school, which leads students through prescribed courses of study that are grounded on one end by the high school curriculum and on the other end by the university curriculum. Suggestions that the Internet will fundamentally change the college experience provide another example. Doucette (1997) speculates about a future in which community colleges may serve an ancillary role to corporate providers of Internet-based instruction; the community college will be a service center, providing counseling, tutoring, and other services for area citizens who take courses offered by Disney, Microsoft, or other for-profit companies. But the notion of college as a *place* for instruction, a notion that is particularly strong among young students who aspire, literally, to "go to college," suggests that traditional classroom instruction will remain an important part of the community college mission (Cohen, 1999).

Work in graded education thus acts as a stabilizing counterweight, lending the community college a predictability that it might not otherwise have were it to abandon schooling for community service. Contracted education, noncredit instruction, Internet courses, and other innovative services for adult learners all have their place in a community-based organization. But in the midst of this ever-shifting instructional landscape, the public knows one thing: the community college is there for young people who continue their education beyond high school. The colleges' continued efforts to monitor student movement from school to college, articulate curricula, and otherwise work with schools to promote student advancement from one grade to the next strengthen that public confidence and enhance the community college's role as a democratizing agent in higher education.

References

Baldwin, A. *Direct Entry Enrollments of Dade County Public, Special, and Private High Schools. Annual Report, Years 1993–94 Through 1997–98.* Miami, Fla.: Miami Dade Community College, 1998. (ED 428 802).

Chenoweth, K. "Thinking K-16." *Black Issues in Higher Education,* Jan. 6, 2000, pp. 14–16.

City College of San Francisco. *San Francisco Unified School District Senior Survey Summary, 1997.* San Francisco: City College of San Francisco, 1999. (ED 433 071)

Cohen, A. M. "What Do Community Colleges Uniquely Provide?" Forum presentation at the Convention of the American Association of Community Colleges, Apr. 7, 1999, Nashville, Tenn.

Conklin, K. A. "Career and Educational Interests of High School Students: A High School-College Collaboration." *Journal of Applied Research in the Community College,* 1996, 4(1), 77–85.

Doucette, D. "What Will Community Colleges Do When Microsoft and Disney Deliver High-Quality, Accredited Higher Education and Training to the Businesses and Homes of Most Americans?" Unpublished paper, 1997. (ED 407 002)

Eaton, J. S., and others. "An Academic Model for Urban Community College Education." *Community, Technical, and Junior College Journal,* 1988, 58(5), 40–43.

Finn, C. E., and Petrilli, M. P. *The State of the Standards 2000.* Washington, D.C.: Thomas B. Fordham Foundation, 2000.

Gerald, D. E., and Hussar, W.J. *Projections of Education Statistics to 2009.* Washington, D.C.: NationalCenter for Education Statistics, 1999. [http://nces.ed.gov/pubs99/ 1999038.pdf].

Gleazer, E. J., Jr. *The Community College: Values, Vision, and Vitality.* Washington, D.C.: American Association of Community and Junior Colleges, 1980.

Holton, J. M. *High School Course Choice, Performance, and Readiness for College. Frederick County Public High School Graduates Enrolling at Frederick Community College.* Frederick, Md.: Frederick Community College, 1998a. (ED 419 569).

Holton, J. M. *Whatever Happened to the Class of 1994? A Three-Year Longitudinal Study of the Traditional Freshmen Entering Frederick Community College in the Fall of 1994.* Frederick, Md.: Frederick Community College, 1998b. (ED 419 568)

Kojaku, L. K., and Nuñez, A.-M. *Descriptive Summary of 1995–96 Beginning Postsecondary Students with Profiles of Students Entering 2- and 4-Year Institutions.* Washington, D.C.: U.S. Department of Education, Office of Educational Research and Improvement, 1999. (ED 425 684)

Langenberg, D. N. *With Renewed Hope—and Determination.* [N.p.]: Maryland Partnership for Teaching and Learning K-16, 1998. [http://mdk16.usmd.edu/aspen2c.html].

McGrath, D., and Van Buskirk, W. *The Collaborative Advantage in Educational Reform: The Case for the K-16 Partnership.* New York: National Center for Educational Alliances, Bronx Community College, 1999.

Merren, J., Hefty, D., and Soto, J. *School to College Linkage—New Models That Work.* Tucson, Ariz.: Pima County Community Coll. District, 1997. (ED 413 967)

Morris, C. *Destination of Dade County Public High School Graduates.* Miami, Fla.: Miami-Dade Community College, 1998. (ED 429 647)

Navarro, M. S., and Natalicio, D. S. "Closing the Achievement Gap in El Paso: A Collaboration for K-12 Renewal." *Phi Delta Kappan,* 1999, *80*(8), 597–601.

O'Banion, T. *A Learning College for a New Century.* Phoenix, Ariz.: American Council on Education and the Oryx Press, 1997.

Oklahoma State Regents for Higher Education. *High School to College-Going Rates: For Oklahoma High School Graduates to Oklahoma Colleges. Linear College-Going Rate, Combined College-Going Rate.* Oklahoma City: Oklahoma State Regents for Higher Education, 1997. (ED 416 792)

Oregon Department of Community Colleges and Workforce Development. *Community College Proficiencies for Entry into Programs.* Salem: Oregon Department of Community Colleges and Workforce Development, 1999. [http://www.odccwd.state.or.us/comcol/prep/PREP.html].

Oregon University System. *Where Have Oregon's Graduates Gone? Survey of the Oregon High School Graduating Class of 1997.* Eugene: Oregon University System, 1998. (ED 430 464).

Oregon University System. *A Brief Overview of the PASS System.* [N.p.]: Oregon University System, 2000a. [http://www.ous.edu/pass/info/about_pass.html].

Oregon University System. *PASS Frequently Asked Questions.* [N.p.]: Oregon University System, 2000b. [http://www.ous.edu/pass/info/faq.html].

Pifer, A. "Community College and Community Leadership." *Community and Junior College Journal,* 1974, *44*(8), 23–26.

Quinley, J. W., and Cantrell, J. E. *Spartanburg Technical College 1998 High School Survey.* Spartanburg, S.C.: Spartanburg Technical College, 1998. (ED 420 333)

Snyder, T., and Hoffman, C. *Digest of Education Statistics 1999.* Washington, D.C.: National Center for Education Statistics, 2000.

Snyder, T. D., Hoffman, C. M., and Geddes, C. M. *Digest of Education Statistics 1996.* Washington, D.C.: National Center for Education Statistics, 1996. [http://nces.ed.gov/pubs/d96/d96t173.html].

Tafel, J., and Eberhart, N. *Statewide School-College (K-16) Partnerships to Improve Student Performance.* Denver, Colo.: State Higher Education Executive Officers, 1999.

U.S. Bureau of the Census. *Statistical Abstract of the United States—1999.* Washington, D.C.: Bureau of the Census, Department of Commerce, 1999.

Windham, P. *Projected Impact of the Baby Boomlet.* Tallahassee: Florida State Board of Community Colleges, 1996. (ED 413 934)

Zeiss, T. *Developing the World's Best Workforce. An Agenda for America's Community Colleges.* Annapolis Junction, Md.: Community College Press, 1997. (ED 407 034)

JAMES C. PALMER is associate professor in the Department of Educational Administration and Foundations, Illinois State University.

11

This *chapter presents an annotated bibliography of
recent ERIC documents that describe the benefits and
pitfalls of collaborations between community colleges
and high schools.*

Sources and Information

Charles L. Outcalt

Both this volume and the educational literature offer examples of successful
partnerships between community colleges and high schools. This chapter
provides an overview of additional case studies from the ERIC database that
describe success stories as well as cautionary tales. These examples demonstrate the need to be sensitive to public perceptions of partnerships and the
limitations of dual-enrollment programs. Most ERIC documents (publications with ED numbers) can be viewed on microfiche at over nine hundred
libraries worldwide. In addition, most may be ordered on microfiche or on
paper from the ERIC Document Reproduction Service (EDRS) by calling
(800)443-ERIC. Journal articles are not available from EDRS, but they can
be acquired through regular library channels or purchased from the University Microfilm International Articles Clearinghouse at (800)521–0600, extension 533.

The Advantages of Collaborative Efforts

Kussrow (1995) provides brief case studies of several innovative North Carolina partnerships between community colleges and high schools and, occa-
sionally, the private sector. This unpublished paper offers a useful discussion
of the rationale and benefits inherent in such joint efforts. Kussrow advises
that successful partnerships must be based on good communication among
all parties. Once effective communication has been established, the community colleges, secondary schools, and other involved organizations can
set mutually agreeable goals. In addition, successful partnerships require
mutual commitment; an appreciation of all parties' resources, needs, and
limitations; clarification of the roles each party will play; and regular assessment of the partnership's ability to meet both its goals and its participants'

needs. Once partnerships become successful, their benefits can include expanded services through more effective use of resources and pooling of expertise, and costs and consequently taxes can be reduced.

Illustrative Case Studies

In addition to the case studies described in this volume, the educational literature offers a wealth of descriptions of exemplary programs.

Marrow and McLaughlin (1995) describe Catonsville Community College's (Maryland) collaboration with government, the private sector, and other educational institutions to meet the local community's educational needs. In this far-ranging partnership, Catonsville Community College (which serves Baltimore) has created a school-to-work consortium involving itself, area high schools, and local businesses, including United Parcel Service (UPS). In addition to the now-common option of dual enrollment in high school and the college, this arrangement provides high school students with a structured work experience and encouragement to continue their education beyond high school. Marrow and McLaughlin include a description of the goals and history of the partnership, an outline of its structure, details on the means by which students are selected, and a description of the benefits that have accrued to UPS, the college, and participating students. These benefits include a better-trained workforce for UPS, increased retention at the college, and improved skills for students. The authors conclude by asserting that community colleges must look for such partnerships with secondary schools and local businesses if they are to continue to evolve and thrive.

Under the Running Start program, created in Washington state in 1990, high school juniors and seniors can take courses, tuition free, at all thirty-two of the state's community and technical colleges. Participants earn both high school and college credit for completing these courses, resulting in a more efficient use of the state's educational resources. Program participation leads to positive educational results for students. For example, participants who transfer to the University of Washington earn higher grade point averages than do their non-Running Start peers. A series of annual reports have documented the program's history, structure, and effects (including transfer rates and student success measures). Crossland (1998) is the most recent of these reports.

Pima (Arizona) Community College's (PCC) very successful and innovative Summer Career Academy creates a link between local K–12 schools, businesses, and PCC by bringing over four hundred students from thirty-six high schools to the college's campus for three-week sessions. PCC ran twenty-one of these sessions in the summer of 1997, focusing on fifteen different occupational areas, including computer science, health care, and emergency services. Program participants are offered a diverse array of instructional opportunities and methods, including a PCC course, field trips, and guest speakers. The program, which was funded by a school-to-work grant, achieved a completion rate of 90.8 percent. Merren, Hefty, and Soto (1997) have included details on program enrollment, an evaluation of specific program offerings, a great many quotations from participants (both positive and constructively critical), a detailed flowchart showing the steps involved in running the program, and recommendations for program improvements. Because of the diversity and candor of these documents, this paper is useful background reading for community college faculty and staff contemplating launching a similar program.

In contrast to the descriptions of single institutions' successes, several ERIC documents provide comprehensive overviews of the efforts of entire state systems to create partnerships between higher education segments, including community colleges and secondary schools. For example, the *College-School Collaborative Activities Report* (1998) reports the results of a survey of collaborations between Maryland's secondary schools and higher education institutions. This study, which examined fourteen community colleges, nine public four-year colleges and universities, and sixteen independent campuses, categorized educational partnerships into six groups: professional development (for instructors at all levels), fieldwork within and outside schools, early intervention, continuing education and teacher training, job training and tech preparation, and distance learning. The study's categorization system could prove useful to those seeking to evaluate the range of offerings within other educational partnerships.

In 1998, Oregon surveyed the extent and nature of its high school students' participation in college courses (Oregon University System, 1999). Overall, approximately sixty-six hundred Oregon high school students were enrolled at some type of higher education institution, with almost half the high schools in the state enrolling their students in community college courses. Larger high schools were more likely to offer dual enrollment or other opportunities (such as college high programs). The report's authors recommended a statewide early options program.

An example of another statewide inventory is provided by Crossland (1998), who outlines the state of Washington's efforts to create collaborations between community colleges and secondary schools, particularly in the area of dual enrollment. The report surveyed the thirty-two community colleges in the state and found that all of them provided advanced placement courses for high school students and offered a tech-prep program; twelve colleges delivered college-level courses in Washington high schools; five colleges accepted high school students into their international baccalaureate programs; and all colleges took part in the state-mandated Running Start program. The report contains detailed survey responses for each of Washington's community colleges, as well as copies of the survey items. Because of these inclusions, Crossland's report is useful for other researchers interested in developing statewide assessments of collaborative programs, especially as they relate to academic cooperation.

Using an even broader focus, Pickeral and Peters (1996) offer a national perspective on the ways in which community colleges can form partnerships with their local communities to create service programs and service-learning opportunities. Their report contains fifteen essays on this topic written by practitioners from across the United States. These essays are not confined to community college–secondary school partnerships; rather they touch on community college collaboration with four-year colleges and universities, and joint efforts between community colleges and the private sector.

Programs Focusing on Special Populations

The ERIC database contains several documents that describe programs designed to benefit members of particular populations. For example, Edwards and others (1996) describe five models for collaborative partnerships meant to serve disadvantaged rural students. Michigan's Saginaw Valley State University uses a variety of techniques to attract and deliver services to a diverse population, including a collaborative program with Delta College. Although some of the programs described involve community college students working with local universities, each contains innovative elements designed to assist underserved rural students.

New Jersey's Faculty Alliance for Education Network (McGrath and Van Buskirk, 1997) was created to link faculty from Essex Community College, two local high schools, and nearby universities, including Rutgers University-Newark and the New Jersey Institute of Technology. Supported by the Ford Foundation's Urban Partnership Program, the alliance, which is dedicated to serving at-risk youth, has established three priorities. First, members worked to smooth articulation policies between Essex Community College and the participating universities, resulting in higher transfer rates. Next, the alliance will turn its attention to strengthening ties between higher education and secondary schools, with the goal of increasing the ability of the participating high schools to act as feeders for the community colleges and universities. The authors provide the results of a qualitative study (interviews with twenty-eight faculty members of the alliance) in which they demonstrate the means by which the success of the first phase of the program led to the creation of the second. The study found that the alliance benefited from several advantages, including long-term funding, an emphasis on the overall mission of the program, contact between program staff and students, and faculty cooperation as teams.

Lessons from the Field on Publicizing and Maintaining Quality Within Collaborative Partnerships

Kiger and Johnson (1997) surveyed forty-seven students who had participated in the dual-enrollment program of an unidentified midwestern community college, as well as fifty-two of these students' parents, to determine how students and parents perceived the program. Students and parents alike thought favorably of the program, but the study revealed that they tended to have different understandings of the benefits of program participation. For students, the dual-enrollment option was an opportunity to experience college life, while for parents it was a means of selecting and preparing for a career. The authors concluded that community colleges must be sensitive to the needs and perceptions of students and their families when planning their dual-enrollment and other educational programs. Although Kiger and Johnson's study included only a comparatively small number of participants from a single institution, it is noteworthy for its inclusion of a marketing perspective that stresses awareness of community beliefs and attitudes.

In contrast to the great majority of sources on community college–secondary school collaboration, Windham (1997) reports the results of somewhat contradictory studies conducted in Florida in the 1990s. She raises the possibility that dual-enrollment programs might not always be successful. Windham cites a 1993 Florida study that found that the vast majority of the state's high school students who had taken chemistry courses in dual-enrollment programs but did not meet standard admissions requirements were forced to retake these courses, resulting in a loss of credits for the students and wasted resources for the state's educational system. As a result of the 1993 study, several Florida community colleges undertook their own evaluation efforts to determine the effectiveness of their dual-enrollment programs. Some of these studies showed that dual-enrollment programs could be successful and lead to positive academic outcomes. For example, Pensacola Junior College (PJC) and Tallahassee Community College (TCC) investigated the academic performance of students who had taken part in dual-enrollment programs in English and history and then transferred to the University of Florida, despite not having met standard admissions requirements to that university. Dual-enrollment students from TCC had slightly higher GPAs than other TCC transfer students, while the University of Florida GPAs of PJC dual-enrollment participants were the same as other PJC transfers. Other statewide studies seemed to contradict the 1993 study as well. For example, a study completed by the state's Community College Board found that very few (140 of 51,382) dual-enrollment courses taken in the 1991–92 academic year had to be repeated between 1992 and 1995. While this figure indicates an extremely low repeat rate, it must be interpreted with some caution, because it reflects only instances in which students repeated exactly the same course they took as dual-enrollment students.

Windham's work reminds us that not all dual-enrollment programs are successful. However, the ERIC documents described in this chapter provide an abundance of programs and models that do provide an opportunity for high schools and community colleges to form collaborative partnerships with one another, with the private sector and with other educational institutions.

References

"College-School Collaborative Activities Report." Unpublished report, Maryland State Higher Education Commission, 1998.

Crossland, R. *Running Start Annual Progress Report, 1996–97.* Washington, D.C.: Washington State Board for Community Technical Colleges, 1998. (ED 416 921)

Edwards, P., and others. "Disadvantaged Rural Students: Five Models of School-University Collaboration." Paper presented at the Seventy-Sixth Annual Meeting of the Association of Teacher Educators, St. Louis, Mo., Feb. 1996. (ED 395 904)

Kiger, D. M., and Johnson, J. A. "Marketing the Perceptions of a Community College's Postsecondary Enrollment Options Program." *Community College Journal of Research and Practice,* 1997, *21*(8), 687–693.

Kussrow, P. G. "Why Community Colleges Need Organizational Partnerships." Unpublished report, 1995. (ED 386 230)

Marrow, A. J., and McLaughlin, J. "Community Collaboration: A Creative Partnership with Catonsville Community College." Paper presented at Leadership 2000, Seventh Annual International Conference of the League for Innovation in the Community College and the Community College Leadership Program, San Francisco, Jul. 1995. (ED 396 796)

McGrath, D., and Van Buskirk, W. *Start with the Faculty.* Newark, N.J.: Newark Faculty Alliance for Education and Systemic Educational Reform, 1997. (ED 416 282)

Merren, J., Hefty, D., and Soto, J. "School to College Linkage—New Models That Work." Paper presented at the Twenty-Third Annual Meeting of the National Council for Occupational Education, San Antonio, Tex., Oct. 1997. (ED 413 967)

Oregon University System. *Oregon Early Options Study.* Eugene: Oregon University System, 1999. (ED 430 470)

Pickeral, T., and Peters, K. (eds.). *Campus Community Collaborations: Examples and Resources for Community Colleges.* Mesa, Ariz.: Campus Compact National Center for Community Colleges, 1996. (ED 405 045)

Windham, P. "High School and Community College Dual Enrollment: Issues of Rigor and Transferability." Unpublished report, Pensacola Junior College, 1997. (ED 413 936)

CHARLES L. OUTCALT *is a Ph.D. candidate in the Graduate School of Education and Information Studies at the University of California, Los Angeles.*

INDEX

Back Issue/Subscription Order Form

Copy or detach and send to:

Jossey-Bass Inc., 350 Sansome Street, San Francisco CA 94104-1342

Call or fax toll free!

Phone 888-378-2537 6AM-5PM PST; Fax 800-605-2665

Back issues: Please send me the following issues at $25 each

(Important: please include series initials and issue number, such as CC90)

1. CC _____

_____

$ _____ Total for single issues

$ _____ Shipping charges (for single issues *only;* subscriptions are exempt from shipping charges): Up to $30, add $5^{50} • $30^{01}–$50, add $6^{50} $50^{01}–$75, add $8 • $75^{01}–$100, add $10 • $100^{01}–$150, add $12 Over $150, call for shipping charge

Subscriptions   Please ❑ start ❑ renew my subscription to *New Directions for Community Colleges* for the year ___ at the following rate:

U.S.:	❑ Individual $60	❑ Institutional $107
Canada:	❑ Individual $85	❑ Institutional $132
All Others:	❑ Individual $90	❑ Institutional $137

NOTE: Subscriptions are quarterly, and are for the calendar year only. Subscriptions begin with the Spring issue of the year indicated above.

$ _____ Total single issues and subscriptions (Add appropriate sales tax for your state for single issue orders. No sales tax for U.S. subscriptions. Canadian residents, add GST for subscriptions and single issues.)

❑ Payment enclosed (U.S. check or money order only)

❑ VISA, MC, AmEx, Discover Card #_____ Exp. date_____

Signature _____ Day phone _____

❑ Bill me (U.S. institutional orders only. Purchase order required)

Purchase order #_____

Federal Tax ID 13559 3032   GST 89102-8052

Name _____

Address _____

_____

Phone_____ E-mail _____

For more information about Jossey-Bass, visit our Web site at:

www.josseybass.com   **PRIORITY CODE = ND1**

OTHER TITLES AVAILABLE IN THE
NEW DIRECTIONS FOR COMMUNITY COLLEGES SERIES
Arthur M. Cohen, Editor-in-Chief
Florence B. Brawer, Associate Editor